Meat &
Potatoes

Table of Contents

Family Favorites

Favorite Beef Stew

Makes 6 to 8 servings

3 carrots, halved and cut into 1-inch pieces
3 stalks celery, cut into 1-inch pieces
2 large potatoes, peeled and cut into ½-inch pieces
1½ cups chopped onions
3 cloves garlic, chopped
4½ teaspoons Worcestershire sauce
¾ teaspoon dried thyme
¾ teaspoon dried basil
½ teaspoon black pepper
1 bay leaf
2 pounds beef stew meat, cut into 1-inch pieces
1 can (about 14 ounces) diced tomatoes
1 can (about 14 ounces) beef broth
½ cup cold water
¼ cup all-purpose flour

SLOW COOKER DIRECTIONS

1. Layer carrots, celery, potatoes, onions, garlic, Worcestershire sauce, thyme, basil, pepper, bay leaf, beef, tomatoes and broth in slow cooker.

2. Cover; cook on LOW 8 to 9 hours.

3. Transfer beef and vegetables to large serving bowl; cover and keep warm. Remove and discard bay leaf.

4. *Turn slow cooker to HIGH.* Stir water into flour in small bowl until smooth. Add ½ cup cooking liquid; mix well. Stir flour mixture into slow cooker. Cover; cook 15 minutes or until thickened. Pour sauce over beef and vegetables. Serve immediately.

Old-Fashioned Chicken with Dumplings
Makes 6 servings

3 to 3½ pounds chicken pieces
3 tablespoons butter
3 cans (about 14 ounces each) chicken broth
3½ cups water
1 teaspoon salt
¼ teaspoon white pepper
2 large carrots, cut into 1-inch slices
2 stalks celery, cut into 1-inch slices
8 to 10 pearl onions, peeled
¼ pound small mushrooms, cut into halves
Parsley Dumplings (recipe follows)
½ cup frozen peas, thawed and drained

1. Brown chicken in butter in 6- to 8-quart saucepan over medium-high heat. Add broth, water, salt and pepper; bring to a boil over high heat. Reduce heat to low. Cover; simmer 15 minutes. Add carrots, celery, onions and mushrooms. Cover; simmer 40 minutes or until chicken and vegetables are tender.

2. Prepare Parsley Dumplings. When chicken is tender, skim fat from broth. Stir in peas. Drop dumpling mixture into broth, making 12 dumplings. Cover; simmer 15 to 20 minutes or until dumplings are firm to the touch and toothpick inserted into centers comes out clean.

Parsley Dumplings: Sift 2 cups all-purpose flour, 4 teaspoons baking powder and 1 teaspoon salt into medium bowl. Cut in 5 tablespoons cold butter until mixture resembles coarse meal. Make well in center; pour in 1 cup milk. Add 2 tablespoons chopped fresh parsley; stir with fork until mixture forms ball.

Old-Fashioned Chicken with Dumplings

London Broil with Marinated Vegetables

Makes 6 servings

¾ cup olive oil
¾ cup red wine
2 tablespoons finely chopped shallots
2 tablespoons red wine vinegar
2 teaspoons minced garlic
½ teaspoon dried thyme
½ teaspoon dried oregano
½ teaspoon dried basil
½ teaspoon black pepper
2 pounds top round London broil (1½ inches thick)
1 red onion, cut into ¼-inch-thick slices
1 package (8 ounces) sliced mushrooms
1 red bell pepper, cut into strips
1 zucchini, cut into ¼-inch-thick slices

1. Whisk olive oil, wine, shallots, vinegar, garlic, thyme, oregano, basil and black pepper in medium bowl.

2. Combine London broil and ¾ cup marinade in large resealable food storage bag. Seal bag; turn to coat. Marinate in refrigerator up to 24 hours, turning bag once or twice.

3. Combine onion, mushrooms, bell pepper, zucchini and remaining marinade in separate large food storage bag. Seal bag; turn to coat. Marinate in refrigerator up to 24 hours, turning bag once or twice.

4. Preheat broiler. Remove beef from marinade and place on broiler pan; discard marinade. Broil 4 to 5 inches from heat about 9 minutes per side or until desired doneness. Let stand 10 minutes before cutting into thin slices.

5. Meanwhile, drain vegetables and arrange on broiler pan; discard marinade. Broil 4 to 5 inches from heat about 9 minutes or until edges of vegetables just begin to brown. Serve vegetables with beef.

London Broil with Marinated Vegetables

Succulent Southern Fried Chicken

Makes 6 servings

1 broiler-fryer chicken (about 3 pounds)
2 tablespoons plus 2 teaspoons Chef Paul Prudhomme's
   Poultry Magic®
2 cups all-purpose flour
2 eggs, beaten well
2 cups milk
   Vegetable oil

Remove excess fat from chicken; cut into 8 pieces (cut breast in half). Season with Poultry Magic®, patting evenly to coat. Place in large resealable plastic bag. Refrigerate overnight.

Remove chicken from refrigerator; let stand at room temperature 10 to 15 minutes. Measure flour into flat pan; reserve. Combine eggs with milk; reserve.

Pour oil to ¾-inch depth into large heavy skillet; heat over high heat to 375°F. (This will take about 13 minutes.)

When oil is hot, and not before, coat half of chicken pieces with flour. Shake off excess; drop chicken pieces into egg mixture. Coat chicken pieces with flour again; shake off excess. Place chicken in single layer in hot oil (cook larger pieces first, skin side down). Adjust heat to maintain 340°F. Turn after about 8 minutes or when chicken is golden brown. Cook about 5 minutes; turn again. (Second turning is to ensure crispiness and crunchiness.) Cook about 3 minutes; remove from skillet and drain on paper towels. Keep warm.

Reheat oil; repeat procedure for second batch. Garnish as desired.

Succulent Southern Fried Chicken

Stuffed Cabbage Rolls

Makes 6 servings

　¾ **pound lean ground beef**
　½ **cup chopped onion**
　1 **cup cooked long grain white rice**
　¼ **teaspoon ground cinnamon**
　　　Salt-free herb seasoning (optional)
　1 **egg white**
12 **large cabbage leaves**
　1 **can (14½ ounces) DEL MONTE® Original Recipe Stewed Tomatoes, No Salt Added**
　1 **can (15 ounces) DEL MONTE® Tomato Sauce, No Salt Added**

1. Brown meat and onion in large skillet over medium-high heat; drain. Add rice and cinnamon. Season with salt-free herb seasoning, if desired.

2. Remove from heat; stir in egg white. Pre-cook cabbage leaves 3 minutes in small amount of boiling water; drain. Divide meat mixture among cabbage leaves. Roll cabbage leaves loosely around meat mixture, allowing room for rice to swell. Secure with toothpicks.

3. Combine undrained tomatoes and tomato sauce in 4-quart saucepan; bring to boil. Reduce heat; add cabbage rolls. Simmer, uncovered, 30 minutes.

Prep Time: 15 minutes ┃ **Cook Time:** 30 minutes

Stuffed Cabbage Rolls

Mustard Crusted Rib Roast

Makes 6 to 8 servings

1 (3-rib) beef rib roast, trimmed* (6 to 7 pounds)
3 tablespoons Dijon mustard
1 tablespoon plus 1½ teaspoons chopped fresh tarragon *or*
     1½ teaspoons dried tarragon
3 cloves garlic, minced
¼ cup dry red wine
⅓ cup finely chopped shallots (about 2 shallots)
1 tablespoon all-purpose flour
1 cup beef broth

*Ask meat retailer to remove chine bone for easier carving. Trim fat to ¼-inch thickness.

1. Preheat oven to 450°F. Place roast, bone side down, in shallow roasting pan. Combine mustard, tarragon and garlic in small bowl; spread over all surfaces of roast, except bottom.

2. *Reduce oven temperature to 350°F.* Roast 2½ to 3 hours or until internal temperature reaches 145°F when tested with meat thermometer inserted into thickest part of roast not touching bone.

3. Transfer roast to cutting board; tent with foil. Let stand 10 to 15 minutes before carving. Internal temperature will continue to rise 5°F to 10°F during stand time.

4. Pour drippings from roasting pan, reserving 1 tablespoon in medium saucepan. Place roasting pan over 2 burners. Add wine to pan; cook over medium heat 2 minutes or until slightly thickened, stirring to scrape up browned bits; set aside.

5. Add shallots to reserved drippings in saucepan; cook and stir over medium heat 4 minutes or until softened. Add flour; cook and stir 1 minute. Add broth and wine mixture; cook 5 minutes or until sauce thickens, stirring occasionally. Pour through strainer into gravy boat; discard solids.

6. Carve roast into ½-inch-thick slices. Serve with gravy.

Mustard Crusted Rib Roast

Sauerbraten with Gingersnap Gravy

Makes 6 to 8 servings

3 cups water
1 cup cider vinegar
1 onion, thinly sliced
3 tablespoons brown sugar
1½ teaspoons salt
2 cloves garlic, crushed
1 teaspoon ground ginger
1 teaspoon whole allspice
1 teaspoon whole cloves
½ teaspoon juniper berries
1 beef rump roast (about 4 pounds)
2 tablespoons vegetable oil
2 tablespoons all-purpose flour
¼ cup crushed gingersnaps

1. Bring water and vinegar to a boil in large saucepan over high heat. Remove from heat; add onion, sugar, salt, garlic, ginger, allspice, cloves and juniper berries. Cool slightly.

2. Place roast in large glass bowl or large resealable food storage bag; pour marinade over roast. Cover or seal bag; marinate in refrigerator at least 8 hours, turning occasionally.

3. Remove roast from marinade, reserving marinade. Pat roast dry with paper towels. Heat oil in Dutch oven over medium-high heat. Brown roast on all sides. Add marinade to Dutch oven. Reduce heat to low. Cover; cook 2½ to 3¼ hours or until fork-tender. Remove roast from Dutch oven; set aside.

4. Strain braising liquid through fine-mesh sieve into large bowl; discard solids. Skim fat from braising liquid; discard. Measure 2 cups braising liquid; discard remaining braising liquid. Place 1½ cups liquid in Dutch oven. Place flour in small bowl; gradually whisk remaining ½ cup braising liquid into flour. Stir into Dutch oven. Add gingersnaps; mix well. Bring to a boil.

5. Return roast to Dutch oven. Reduce heat to low. Cover; cook 15 to 20 minutes until flavors blend and sauce thickens. Slice roast and serve with sauce.

Sauerbraten with Gingersnap Gravy

Crispy Ranch Chicken

Makes 6 servings

1½ cups cornflake crumbs
1 teaspoon dried rosemary
½ teaspoon salt
½ teaspoon black pepper
1½ cups ranch salad dressing
3 pounds chicken pieces

1. Preheat oven to 375°F. Spray 13×9-inch baking dish with nonstick cooking spray. Combine cornflakes, rosemary, salt and pepper in medium bowl.

2. Pour salad dressing in separate medium bowl. Dip chicken pieces in salad dressing, coating well. Dredge coated chicken in crumb mixture.

3. Place chicken in prepared baking dish. Bake 50 to 55 minutes or until cooked through (165°F). Serve with desired side dishes.

Cook's Nook: To add an Italian flair to this dish, try substituting 1½ cups Italian-seasoned dry bread crumbs and ½ cup grated Parmesan cheese for the cornflake crumbs, rosemary, salt and pepper. Prepare recipe as directed.

Crispy Ranch Chicken

Marvelous Meat Loaf

Makes 6 to 8 servings

1 pound lean ground beef
½ pound spicy bulk pork sausage
¾ cup fresh bread crumbs
2 eggs
¾ cup ketchup, divided
½ cup finely chopped onion
½ cup shredded carrots
3 teaspoons chili powder, divided
¾ teaspoon salt

1. Preheat oven to 375°F. Combine beef, sausage, bread crumbs, eggs, ¼ cup ketchup, onion, carrots, 2 teaspoons chili powder and salt in large bowl. Mix well and press into 9×5-inch loaf pan.

2. Combine remaining ½ cup ketchup and 1 teaspoon chili powder in small bowl; spread over top of loaf.

3. Bake 1 hour or until internal temperature of loaf reaches 165°F. Let stand 5 minutes before slicing.

Marvelous Meat Loaf

Italian Meatballs

Makes 5 to 6 servings

1½ pounds meat loaf mix* or lean ground beef
⅓ cup dry bread crumbs
⅓ cup grated onion
⅓ cup milk
¼ cup (1 ounce) freshly grated Parmesan cheese
1 egg
2 cloves garlic, minced
1½ teaspoons dried basil
1 teaspoon salt
1 teaspoon dried oregano
½ teaspoon dried sage
¼ teaspoon red pepper flakes
  Marinara Sauce (page 21)
  Additional grated Parmesan cheese
  Hot cooked spaghetti (optional)

Meat loaf mix is a combination of 1 pound ground beef, ¼ pound pork and ¼ pound veal.

1. Preheat oven to 400°F. Spray broiler pan with nonstick cooking spray. Combine all ingredients except Marinara Sauce, additional cheese and pasta in large bowl. Mix lightly but thoroughly. Shape to form meatballs using ⅓ cup.

2. Place meatballs on prepared pan; bake 25 to 30 minutes or until thermometer inserted into centers registers 145°F.

3. Meanwhile, prepare Marinara Sauce. Add cooked meatballs to Marinara Sauce; simmer about 10 minutes or until meatballs are cooked through and internal temperature reaches 165°F.

4. Serve meatballs in shallow bowls over spaghetti; top with sauce. Serve with additional cheese, if desired.

Marinara Sauce

Makes about 3½ cups

1½ tablespoons olive oil
3 cloves garlic, minced
1 can (28 ounces) Italian plum tomatoes, undrained
¼ cup tomato paste
2 teaspoons dried basil
½ teaspoon sugar
¼ teaspoon salt
¼ teaspoon red pepper flakes

Heat oil in large saucepan over medium heat. Add garlic; cook and stir 3 minutes. Stir in remaining ingredients. Bring to a boil. Reduce heat to low; simmer, uncovered, 10 minutes.

Tip: Make a double or triple batch of this sauce and freeze the rest for a quick and easy pasta night!

Pot Roast Carbonnade

Makes 8 servings

**6 thick slices applewood-smoked or other smoked bacon
(about 6 ounces)**
2 tablespoons all-purpose flour
¾ teaspoon salt
½ teaspoon black pepper
1 beef chuck arm pot roast* (about 3½ pounds)
3 large Spanish onions (about 2 pounds), thinly sliced
2 tablespoons light brown sugar
1 can (about 14 ounces) beef broth
1 bottle (12 ounces) beer (not dark)
2 teaspoons dried thyme
2 bay leaves
Boiled potatoes (optional)
Additional black pepper (optional)

**A well-trimmed, 3-pound boneless beef chuck shoulder pot roast can be substituted;
however, the bone in the chuck arm roast will give the sauce more flavor.*

1. Preheat oven to 350°F. Cook bacon in Dutch oven over medium heat until crisp. Drain bacon on paper towels, reserving drippings in Dutch oven. Set bacon aside.

2. Combine flour, salt and ½ teaspoon pepper in small bowl; spread on sheet of waxed paper. Place pot roast on flour mixture; roll to coat well. Place pot roast in drippings in Dutch oven. Brown over medium-low heat about 4 to 5 minutes per side. Remove to platter.

3. Pour off all but 2 tablespoons drippings from Dutch oven. Add onions to drippings; cover and cook 10 minutes over medium heat, stirring once. Sprinkle with sugar; cook and stir onions over medium-high heat 10 minutes or until golden brown and tender.

4. Add broth, beer, thyme and bay leaves to Dutch oven; bring to a boil. Return pot roast with any accumulated juices to Dutch oven. Remove from heat; spoon sauce over top. Cover; bake 2 hours or until meat is fork-tender.

continued on page 24

Pot Roast Carbonnade

Pot Roast Carbonnade, continued

5. Transfer meat to cutting board; tent with foil.

6. Remove and discard bay leaves. Skim fat from juices. Place half of juice mixture in food processor; process until smooth. Repeat with remaining juice mixture; return mixture to Dutch oven. Crumble bacon; stir into sauce. Cook over medium heat until heated through.

7. Discard bone from roast; carve roast into ¼-inch-thick slices with carving knife. Spoon sauce over roast. Serve roast with boiled potatoes and additional pepper.

Harvest Ham Supper
Makes 6 servings

6 carrots, cut into 2-inch pieces
3 medium sweet potatoes, quartered
1 to 1½ pounds boneless ham
1 cup maple syrup

SLOW COOKER DIRECTIONS

1. Place carrots and potatoes in bottom of slow cooker. Place ham on top of vegetables. Pour syrup over ham and vegetables.

2. Cover; cook on LOW 6 to 8 hours.

Prep Time: 10 minutes | **Cook Time:** 6 to 8 hours

Harvest Ham Supper

Harvest Pot Roast with Sweet Potatoes

Makes 6 servings

4 large sweet potatoes, peeled, if desired, and cut into large chunks
3- to 3½-pound boneless pot roast (rump, chuck or round)
1 envelope LIPTON® RECIPE SECRETS® Onion Soup Mix
1½ cups water
¼ cup soy sauce
2 tablespoons firmly packed dark brown sugar
1 teaspoon ground ginger (optional)
3 tablespoons water
2 tablespoons all-purpose flour

SLOW COOKER DIRECTIONS

1. In slow cooker, add potatoes, then roast. Combine LIPTON® RECIPE SECRETS® Onion Soup Mix, 1½ cups water, soy sauce, brown sugar and ginger, if desired; pour over roast.

2. Cook, covered, on LOW 8 to 10 hours or on HIGH 4 to 6 hours, or until roast is tender.

3. Remove roast and potatoes to serving platter. Blend 3 tablespoons water with flour and stir into juices in slow cooker. Cook, covered, on HIGH 15 minutes or until thickened.

Prep Time: 10 minutes | **Cook Time:** 4 hours, 15 minutes (HIGH)

Harvest Pot Roast With Sweet Potatoes

Fire Up the Grill

Spicy Smoked Beef Ribs

Makes 4 to 6 servings

   4 to 6 pounds beef back ribs, cut into 3- to 4-rib pieces
      Black pepper
1⅓ cups barbecue sauce
   2 teaspoons hot pepper sauce or Szechwan chili sauce
   4 wood chunks for smoking
      Beer at room temperature or warm water

1. Spread ribs on baking sheet; season with black pepper. Combine barbecue sauce and hot pepper sauce in small bowl. Brush ribs with half of sauce. Marinate in refrigerator 30 minutes to 1 hour.

2. Meanwhile, soak wood chunks in water at least 30 minutes; drain.

3. Prepare grill for indirect cooking. Add soaked wood to fire. Place foil drip pan in center of grill. Fill pan half full with beer.

4. Grease grid. Place ribs on grid, meaty side up, directly above drip pan. Grill ribs over low heat, covered, about 1 hour or until meat is tender, brushing remaining sauce over ribs 2 or 3 times during cooking. (If grill has thermometer, maintain cooking temperature between 250°F to 275°F. Add a few more briquets as needed to maintain constant temperature.) Add more soaked wood chips after 30 minutes, if necessary.

Honey and Mustard Glazed Chicken

Makes 4 to 5 servings

1 whole chicken (4 to 5 pounds), giblets removed
1 tablespoon vegetable oil
¼ cup honey
2 tablespoons Dijon mustard
1 tablespoon reduced-sodium soy sauce
½ teaspoon ground ginger
⅛ teaspoon black pepper

1. Prepare grill for indirect cooking.

2. Pull chicken skin over neck; secure with metal skewer. Tuck wings under back; tie legs together with wet string. Lightly brush chicken with oil.

3. Combine honey, mustard, soy sauce, ginger and pepper in small bowl; set aside.

4. Place chicken, breast side up, on grid directly over drip pan. Grill, covered, over medium-high heat 1 hour 30 minutes or until cooked through (165°F) for both light and dark meat. Brush with honey mixture every 10 minutes during last 30 minutes of cooking time.*

5. Transfer chicken to cutting board; tent with foil. Let stand 15 minutes before carving.

If using grill with heat on one side (rather than around drip pan), rotate chicken 180 degrees after 45 minutes of cooking time.

Honey and Mustard Glazed Chicken

Spice-Rubbed Beef Brisket

Makes 12 servings

  2 cups hickory chips
  1 teaspoon salt
  1 teaspoon paprika
  1 teaspoon chili powder
  1 teaspoon garlic pepper
  1 beef brisket (3 to 3½ pounds)
  ¼ cup beer or beef broth
  1 tablespoon Worcestershire sauce
  1 tablespoon balsamic vinegar
  1 teaspoon olive oil
  ¼ teaspoon dry mustard
  6 ears corn, cut into 2-inch pieces
 12 small new potatoes
  6 carrots, cut into 2-inch pieces
  2 green bell peppers, cut into 2-inch squares
  6 tablespoons lemon juice
  6 tablespoons water
 1½ teaspoons Italian seasoning

1. Soak hickory chips in water 30 minutes. Prepare grill for indirect cooking. Bank briquets on either side of water-filled drip pan.

2. Combine salt, paprika, chili powder and garlic pepper in small bowl. Rub spice mixture onto both sides of brisket; cover and set aside. Combine beer, Worcestershire sauce, vinegar, oil and dry mustard in small bowl; set aside.

3. Drain hickory chips; sprinkle ½ cup over coals. Place brisket on grid directly over drip pan. Cover; grill over medium coals 30 minutes. Baste with reserved beer mixture. Grill 3 hours, turning every 30 minutes or until 160°F. (Add briquets and hickory chips to each side of fire every hour.)

4. Meanwhile, thread corn, potatoes, carrots and bell peppers onto metal skewers. Combine lemon juice, water and Italian seasoning in small bowl; brush onto vegetables. Grill vegetables 20 to 25 minutes or until tender.

5. Remove brisket to cutting board; tent loosely with foil. Let stand 10 minutes before carving. Remove excess fat. Serve beef with vegetable kabobs.

Spice-Rubbed Beef Brisket

Glazed Ham and Sweet Potato Kabobs

Makes 4 servings

  1 sweet potato (about 12 ounces), peeled
¼ cup water
¼ cup packed dark brown sugar
¼ cup (½ stick) butter
  2 tablespoons cider vinegar
  2 tablespoons molasses
  1 tablespoon yellow mustard
  1 tablespoon Worcestershire sauce
¾ teaspoon ground cinnamon
½ teaspoon ground allspice
⅛ teaspoon red pepper flakes
  1 boneless ham slice (about 12 ounces), ¼ inch thick, cut into 20 cubes
16 fresh pineapple chunks (about 1 inch)
  1 package (10 ounces) mixed salad greens

1. Grease grid. Prepare grill for direct cooking over medium heat. Soak 4 (12-inch) wooden skewers in water 20 minutes.

2. Meanwhile, cut sweet potato into 16 pieces; place in shallow microwavable dish with ¼ cup water. Cover; microwave on HIGH 4 minutes or until fork-tender. Drain. Spread potatoes in single layer; cool 5 minutes.

3. Combine brown sugar, butter, vinegar, molasses, mustard, Worcestershire sauce, cinnamon, allspice and red pepper flakes in large saucepan. Bring to a boil over high heat. Reduce heat to medium-high; cook 2 minutes or until sauce reduces to ½ cup. Remove from heat; cool slightly.

4. Thread ham, potato and pineapple onto prepared skewers, starting and ending with ham.

5. Arrange skewers on grid. Grill 6 to 8 minutes, turning every 2 minutes and brushing with glaze until potatoes are brown and ham is heated through. Cover; let stand 5 minutes.

6. Place salad greens on platter. Remove ham, sweet potato and pineapple from skewers; arrange on top of greens. Serve immediately.

Glazed Ham and Sweet Potato Kabobs

Seasoned Baby Back Ribs
Makes 6 servings

1 tablespoon paprika
1½ teaspoons garlic salt
1 teaspoon celery salt
½ teaspoon black pepper
¼ teaspoon ground red pepper
4 pounds pork baby back ribs, cut into 3- to 4-rib portions, well trimmed
Barbecue Sauce (recipe follows)

1. Preheat oven to 350°F.

2. Combine paprika, garlic salt, celery salt, black pepper and red pepper in small bowl. Rub over all surfaces of ribs.

3. Place ribs in foil-lined shallow roasting pan. Bake 30 minutes.

4. Meanwhile, prepare grill for direct cooking. Prepare Barbecue Sauce; set aside.

5. Place ribs directly on grid. Cover; grill over medium coals 10 minutes.

6. Brush ribs with half of Barbecue Sauce. Cover; grill 10 minutes or until ribs are tender and browned. Serve with reserved sauce.

Barbecue Sauce
Makes about ⅓ cup

½ cup ketchup
⅓ cup packed light brown sugar
1 tablespoon cider vinegar
2 teaspoons Worcestershire sauce
1 teaspoon soy sauce

Combine all ingredients in glass measuring cup or small bowl. Reserve half of sauce for serving.

Seasoned Baby Back Ribs

Chicken and Bacon Skewers

Makes 2 servings

¼ **cup lemon juice**
¼ **cup soy sauce**
2 **tablespoons brown sugar**
1½ **teaspoons lemon pepper**
2 **boneless skinless chicken breasts (about ½ pound), cut into**
  1-inch cubes
1 **teaspoon coarsely ground black pepper**
½ **pound bacon slices, cut in half crosswise**

1. Combine lemon juice, soy sauce, brown sugar and lemon pepper in large resealable food storage bag; mix well. Remove ¼ cup marinade; set aside. Add chicken to bag; seal. Marinate in refrigerator at least 30 minutes. Soak 4 (12-inch) wooden skewers in water 20 minutes.

2. Sprinkle black pepper over top sides of bacon; gently press to adhere. Remove chicken from bag; discard marinade. Alternately thread chicken and bacon onto skewers.

3. Grill skewers, turning occasionally, 10 to 15 minutes or until chicken is no longer pink in center and bacon is crisp. Brush several times with reserved marinade.

Chicken and Bacon Skewers

Chipotle-Marinated Beef Flank Steak

Makes 4 to 6 servings

**1 beef flank steak (about 1½ to 2 pounds) or beef top round steak,
cut 1 inch thick (about 1¾ pounds)**
Salt

MARINADE
⅓ cup fresh lime juice
¼ cup chopped fresh cilantro
1 tablespoon packed brown sugar
2 teaspoons minced chipotle chilies in adobo sauce
2 tablespoons adobo sauce (from chilies)
2 cloves garlic, minced
1 teaspoon freshly grated lime peel

1. Combine marinade ingredients in small bowl; mix well. Place beef steak and marinade in food-safe plastic bag; turn steak to coat. Close bag securely and marinate in refrigerator 6 hours or as long as overnight.

2. Remove steak from marinade; discard marinade. Place steak on grid over medium, ash-covered coals. Grill flank steak, uncovered, 17 to 21 minutes for medium rare (145°F) to medium (160°F) doneness (top round steak 16 to 18 minutes for medium rare doneness; do not overcook), turning occasionally. Carve steak across the grain into thin slices. Season with salt, as desired.

Cook's Tip: To broil, place steak on rack in broiler pan so surface of beef is 2 to 3 inches from heat. Broil flank steak 13 to 18 minutes for medium-rare to medium doneness (top round steak 17 to 18 minutes for medium rare doneness; do not overcook), turning once.

Cook's Tip: To prepare on gas grill, preheat grill according to manufacturer's directions for medium heat. Grill flank steak, covered, 16 to 21 minutes for medium rare (145°F) to medium (160°F) doneness (top round steak 16 to 19 minutes for medium rare doneness; do not overcook), turning occasionally.

Prep and Cook Time: 30 minutes I **Marinate Time:** 6 hours or overnight

Favorite recipe from *Courtesy The Beef Checkoff*

Chipotle-Marinated Beef Flank Steak

Meaty Chili Dogs
Makes 12 servings

1 pound ground beef
¼ pound Italian sausage, casings removed
1 large onion, chopped
2 medium stalks celery, diced
1 jalapeño pepper,* seeded and chopped
2 cloves garlic, minced
1 tablespoon chili powder
2 teaspoons sugar
1 can (28 ounces) diced tomatoes
1 can (about 15 ounces) pinto beans, rinsed and drained
1 can (12 ounces) tomato juice
1 cup water
12 hot dogs
12 hot dog buns, split and toasted

*Jalapeño peppers can sting and irritate the skin, so wear rubber gloves when handling peppers and do not touch your eyes.

1. Cook beef, sausage, onion, celery, jalapeño and garlic in 5-quart Dutch oven over medium heat until meat is cooked through and onion is tender, stirring to break up meat. Drain fat.

2. Stir in chili powder and sugar. Add tomatoes, beans, tomato juice and water. Bring to a boil over high heat. Reduce heat to low; simmer 30 minutes, stirring occasionally.

3. Prepare grill for direct cooking. Arrange hot dogs on grid directly above medium-hot coals. Grill 5 to 8 minutes or until heated through, turning often. Place hot dogs in buns. Spoon about ¼ cup chili over each.

Meaty Chili Dog

Spicy Grilled Chicken

Makes 4 servings

4 boneless skinless chicken breasts
2 tablespoons minced garlic
1 tablespoon salt
1 tablespoon red pepper flakes
2 teaspoons paprika
2 teaspoons black pepper

1. Prepare grill for direct cooking over medium-high heat. Lightly score each chicken breast 3 or 4 times with knife.

2. Combine garlic, salt, red pepper flakes, paprika and black pepper in small shallow bowl. Coat both sides of chicken with garlic mixture.

3. Grill chicken 8 to 10 minutes or until chicken is no longer pink in center, turning once.

Serving Suggestion: Excellent served with rice pilaf.

Spicy Grilled Chicken

Honey-Lemon Glazed Veal Chops

Makes 4 servings

½ **teaspoon grated lemon peel**
3 **tablespoons lemon juice**
2 **tablespoons honey**
2 **teaspoons grated fresh ginger**
1 **teaspoon Dijon mustard**
4 **veal rib chops, cut 1-inch thick (about 8 ounces each)**

1. Combine lemon peel, lemon juice, honey, ginger and mustard in large resealable food storage bag. Place veal in bag, turning to thoroughly coat with marinade. Marinate in refrigerator 30 minutes. Prepare grill for direct cooking.

2. Remove chops from bag. Place chops on grid over medium coals. Brush with any remaining marinade. Grill 12 to 14 minutes for medium (160°F) or to desired doneness, turning once.

Prep Time: 10 minutes | **Cook Time:** 12 to 14 minutes

 Tip: To check temperature of coals, cautiously hold the palm of your hand about 4 inches above coals. Count the number of seconds you can hold it in that position before the heat forces you to pull it away (about 4 seconds for medium coals is normal).

Honey-Lemon Glazed Veal Chop

Peppered Beef Ribeye Roast
Makes 6 to 8 servings

1½ tablespoons black peppercorns
1 boneless beef ribeye roast (about 2½ to 3 pounds), well trimmed
¼ cup Dijon mustard
2 cloves garlic, minced
Sour Cream Sauce (recipe follows)

1. Prepare grill for indirect cooking over medium heat with drip pan in center.

2. Place peppercorns in small resealable food storage bag. Squeeze out excess air; close bag securely. Pound peppercorns using flat side of meat mallet or rolling pin until cracked.

3. Pat roast dry with paper towels. Combine mustard and garlic in small bowl; spread over roast. Sprinkle with pepper.

4. Place roast on grid directly over drip pan. Grill, covered, 1 hour or until 145°F or desired doneness. (If using charcoal grill, add 4 to 9 briquets to both sides of the fire after 45 minutes to maintain medium heat.)

5. Meanwhile, prepare Sour Cream Sauce. Cover; refrigerate until serving.

6. Transfer roast to cutting board; tent with foil. Let stand 10 to 15 minutes before carving. Serve with Sour Cream Sauce.

Sour Cream Sauce
Makes about 1 cup

¾ cup sour cream
2 tablespoons prepared horseradish
1 tablespoon balsamic vinegar
½ teaspoon sugar

Combine all ingredients in small bowl; mix well.

Peppered Beef Ribeye Roast

Quick and Easy

Corned Beef Hash

Makes 4 servings

  2 large russet potatoes, peeled and cut into ½-inch cubes
½ teaspoon salt
¼ teaspoon black pepper
¼ cup (½ stick) butter or margarine
  1 cup chopped onion
½ pound corned beef, finely chopped
  1 tablespoon horseradish
  4 eggs

1. Place potatoes in large skillet; cover with water. Bring to a boil over high heat. Reduce heat to low; simmer 6 minutes. (Potatoes will be firm.) Remove potatoes from skillet; drain well. Sprinkle with salt and pepper.

2. Melt butter in same skillet over medium heat. Add onion; cook and stir 5 minutes. Stir in corned beef, horseradish and potatoes; mix well. Press mixture with spatula to flatten.

3. Reduce heat to low. Cook 10 to 15 minutes. Turn mixture in large pieces; pat down and cook 10 to 15 minutes or until bottom is well browned.

4. Meanwhile, bring 1 inch water to a simmer in small saucepan. Break 1 egg into shallow dish; carefully slide into water. Cook 5 minutes or until whites are opaque. Remove with slotted spoon to plate; keep warm. Repeat with remaining eggs.

5. Top each serving hash with 1 poached egg. Serve immediately.

Bratwurst Skillet

Makes 4 servings

    1 pound bratwurst links, cut into ½-inch slices
1½ cups sliced onions
1½ cups green bell pepper strips
1½ cups red bell pepper strips
    1 teaspoon paprika
    1 teaspoon caraway seeds

1. Heat large skillet over medium heat. Add bratwurst; cover and cook about 5 minutes or until browned and no longer pink in center. Transfer bratwurst to plate. Cover and keep warm.

2. Drain all but 1 tablespoon drippings from skillet. Add onions, bell peppers, paprika and caraway seeds. Cook and stir about 5 minutes or until vegetables are tender. Return bratwurst to skillet. Serve immediately.

Prep and Cook Time: 18 minutes

Tip: Bratwurst is a German sausage usually made of pork and veal that is seasoned with a variety of spices including ginger, nutmeg and caraway. Precooked varieties are available, but most are found fresh and must be cooked thoroughly before eating.

Bratwurst Skillet

Roast Pork Chops with Apple and Cabbage

Makes 4 servings

3 teaspoons olive oil, divided
½ medium onion, thinly sliced
1 teaspoon dried thyme
2 cloves garlic, minced
4 pork chops (6 to 8 ounces each), 1 inch thick
  Salt
¼ teaspoon black pepper, plus additional to taste
¼ cup cider vinegar
1 tablespoon packed brown sugar
1 large McIntosh apple, peeled and chopped
½ (8-ounce) package shredded coleslaw mix

1. Preheat over to 375°F.

2. Heat 2 teaspoons oil in large ovenproof skillet over medium-high heat. Add onion; cook, covered, 4 to 6 minutes or until tender, stirring often. Add thyme and garlic; cook and stir 30 seconds. Transfer to small bowl; set aside.

3. Add remaining 1 teaspoon oil to same skillet. Season pork chops with salt and pepper. Place in skillet; cook 2 minutes on each side or until browned. Remove pork chops from skillet; set aside.

4. Remove skillet from heat. Add vinegar, brown sugar and ¼ teaspoon pepper; stir to dissolve sugar and scrape up browned bits. Add onion mixture, apple and coleslaw mix; do not stir.

5. Arrange pork chops on top of cabbage mixture, overlapping to fit. Cover skillet; place in oven. Bake 15 minutes or until pork chops are just barely pink in center.

 Tip: This recipe can be made up to a day ahead. Prepare and separately wrap pork chops and cabbage-apple mixture. Refrigerate until ready to serve. Preheat oven to 375°F. Cook and stir cabbage mixture in large ovenproof skillet over medium-high heat until blended and liquid comes to a boil. Lay pork chops on top of cabbage mixture, overlapping to fit. Continue as directed in recipe.

Roast Pork Chop with Apple and Cabbage

Ham & Barbecued Bean Skillet

Makes 4 servings

1 tablespoon vegetable oil
1 cup chopped onion
1 teaspoon minced garlic
1 can (about 15 ounces) kidney beans, rinsed and drained
1 can (about 15 ounces) cannellini or Great Northern beans, rinsed
    and drained
1 cup chopped green bell pepper
½ cup packed light brown sugar
½ cup ketchup
2 tablespoons cider vinegar
2 teaspoons dry mustard
1 ham steak (½ inch thick, about 12 ounces), cut into ½-inch pieces

1. Heat oil in large deep skillet over medium-high heat. Add onion and garlic; cook and stir 3 minutes. Add kidney beans, cannellini beans, bell pepper, brown sugar, ketchup, vinegar and mustard; mix well.

2. Add ham to skillet. Reduce heat to low; simmer 5 minutes or until sauce thickens and mixture is heated through, stirring occasionally.

Prep and Cook Time: 20 minutes

Ham & Barbecued Bean Skillet

All-in-One Burger Stew

Makes 6 servings

1 pound ground beef
2 cups frozen Italian-style vegetables
1 can (about 14 ounces) diced tomatoes with basil and garlic
1 can (about 14 ounces) beef broth
2½ cups uncooked medium egg noodles
Salt and black pepper

1. Brown beef in Dutch oven or large skillet over medium-high heat 6 to 8 minutes, stirring to break up meat. Drain fat.

2. Add vegetables, tomatoes and broth; bring to a boil over high heat.

3. Add noodles; reduce heat to medium. Cover; cook 12 to 15 minutes or until noodles and vegetables are tender. Season with salt and pepper.

Note: For a special touch, sprinkle with chopped parsley before serving.

Prep and Cook Time: 25 minutes

Tip: To complete this meal, serve with breadsticks or a loaf of Italian bread and a simple salad.

All-in-One Burger Stew

Nutty Oven-Fried Chicken Drumsticks

Makes 4 to 6 servings

12 chicken drumsticks *or* **6** legs (about **3** pounds)
  1 egg, beaten
  1 cup cornflake crumbs
  ⅓ cup finely chopped pecans
  1 tablespoon sugar
1½ teaspoons salt
  ½ teaspoon onion powder
  ½ teaspoon black pepper
  ¼ cup (½ stick) butter or margarine, melted

1. Preheat oven to 400°F. Line baking sheet with foil and spray with nonstick cooking spray. Toss chicken with egg to coat.

2. Combine cornflake crumbs, pecans, sugar, salt, onion powder and pepper in large resealable food storage bag. Add chicken, two pieces at a time; shake to coat.

3. Place chicken on prepared baking sheet; drizzle with butter. Bake 40 to 45 minutes or until cooked through (165°F).

Skillet Sausage with Potatoes and Rosemary

Makes 4 to 6 servings

1 tablespoon vegetable oil
3 cups diced red skin potatoes
1 cup diced onion
1 pound BOB EVANS® Original Recipe Roll Sausage
½ teaspoon dried rosemary
¼ teaspoon rubbed sage
   Salt and black pepper to taste
2 tablespoons chopped fresh parsley

Heat oil in large skillet over medium-high heat 1 minute. Add potatoes; cook 5 to 10 minutes or until slightly brown, stirring occasionally. Add onion; cook until tender. Add crumbled sausage; cook until browned. Add rosemary, sage, salt and pepper; cook and stir until well blended. Transfer to serving platter and garnish with parsley. Refrigerate leftovers.

Beef Stroganoff
Makes 4 servings

8 ounces uncooked egg noodles
¼ cup all-purpose flour
½ teaspoon salt
¼ teaspoon black pepper
1¼ pounds beef tenderloin steaks or tenderloin tips
4 tablespoons butter, divided
¾ cup chopped onion
12 ounces fresh button mushrooms, sliced
1 can (10½ ounces) condensed beef broth
2 tablespoons tomato paste
1 tablespoon Worcestershire sauce
1 cup sour cream, at room temperature
Fresh chives (optional)

1. Cook noodles according to package directions; drain and keep warm.

2. Meanwhile, combine flour, salt and pepper in large resealable food storage bag. Cut steaks into 1½×½-inch strips; add half of beef to flour mixture. Seal bag; shake to coat. Repeat with remaining beef. Discard flour mixture.

3. Melt 1 tablespoon butter in large nonstick skillet over medium-high heat. Add half of beef to skillet; cook and stir until browned on all sides. *Do not overcook.* Transfer to medium bowl. Repeat with 1 tablespoon butter and remaining beef.

4. Melt remaining 2 tablespoons butter in same skillet over medium-high heat. Add onion; cook and stir 5 minutes. Add mushrooms; cook and stir 5 minutes or until mushrooms are tender.

5. Add broth, tomato paste and Worcestershire sauce; bring to a boil, stirring to scrape up browned bits.

6. Return beef and any accumulated juices to skillet; cook about 5 minutes or until heated through and sauce is thickened. Stir in sour cream; heat through. *Do not boil.*

7. Serve beef mixture over noodles. Garnish with chives.

Beef Stroganoff

Easy Santa Fe Style Stuffed Peppers

Makes 4 servings

1 cup MINUTE® Brown Rice, uncooked
    Nonstick cooking spray
1 pound lean ground beef*
1 package (10 ounces) frozen whole-kernel corn
1½ cups chunky salsa
4 large red bell peppers, tops and seeds removed**
1 cup Colby and Monterey Jack cheese, shredded

*Or substitute ground turkey.
**Or substitute green, yellow or orange bell peppers.

Prepare rice according to package directions.

Preheat oven to 425°F.

Spray large nonstick skillet with nonstick cooking spray. Add beef and brown over medium heat; drain excess fat. Stir in corn, salsa and rice.

Pierce bell peppers with fork or sharp knife; place in baking dish. Fill peppers with meat mixture. Cover with foil.

Bake 20 minutes. Uncover. Sprinkle with cheese before serving.

Tip: If softer peppers are desired, reduce the oven temperature to 375°F and cook the filled peppers, covered, for 1 hour.

Easy Santa Fe Style Stuffed Peppers

Honeyed Harvest Chicken

Makes 4 servings

1 sweet potato (about 12 ounces)
4 bone-in chicken breasts
   Salt and black pepper
1 tablespoon olive oil
2 apples, peeled, cored and cut into wedges
¾ cup chicken broth
½ cup dried cranberries
2 tablespoons honey
2 teaspoons lemon juice
⅛ teaspoon ground red pepper
   Hot cooked rice

1. Pierce sweet potato in several places with fork. Microwave on HIGH 5 minutes. Let stand 10 minutes. Peel; cut into 1-inch pieces. Season chicken with salt and black pepper.

2. Heat oil in large skillet over medium-high heat. Add chicken; cook 4 minutes on each side or until brown. Remove chicken to plate; keep warm.

3. Add sweet potato and apples to skillet; cook and stir 2 minutes. Add broth, cranberries, honey, lemon juice and red pepper. Bring to a boil; simmer 2 minutes, stirring occasionally. Return chicken to skillet; simmer 10 minutes or until liquid is thickened and chicken is cooked through (165°F).

Honeyed Harvest Chicken

Ham and Sweet Potato Skillet

Makes 4 servings

2 sweet potatoes (about 1¼ pounds)
3 cups water
1 tablespoon salt
1 fully cooked ham steak (about 1 pound)
½ cup brewed coffee
¼ cup pure maple syrup
2 tablespoons butter
½ cup coarsely chopped pecans, toasted*

*To toast pecans, place in a nonstick skillet. Cook and stir over medium-low heat about 5 minutes or until pecans begin to brown. Remove immediately to a plate to cool.

1. Peel sweet potatoes; cut into ¾-inch pieces. Combine water and salt in large saucepan over medium heat. Add sweet potatoes; simmer 8 to 10 minutes or until almost tender. Drain well.

2. Meanwhile, cut ham into ¾-inch chunks; discard bone and fat.

3. Combine coffee, maple syrup and butter in large skillet. Bring to a boil over high heat. Reduce heat to medium-low; simmer 3 minutes. Add sweet potatoes and ham; simmer until ham is heated through and sauce is bubbly and slightly thickened, stirring occasionally. Sprinkle with pecans just before serving.

Ham and Sweet Potato Skillet

Herbed Beef & Vegetable Skillet

Makes 4 servings

2 tablespoons vegetable or canola oil
1 pound boneless beef sirloin or top round steak, ¾-inch thick, cut
    into thin strips
3 medium carrots, sliced thin diagonally (about 1½ cups)
1 medium onion, chopped (about ½ cup)
2 cloves garlic, minced
½ teaspoon dried thyme leaves, crushed
1 can (10¾ ounces) CAMPBELL'S® Condensed Golden Mushroom Soup
¼ cup water
2 teaspoons Worcestershire sauce
⅛ teaspoon ground black pepper
   Hot cooked noodles

1. Heat **1 tablespoon** of the oil in a 12-inch skillet over medium-high heat. Add the beef and cook and stir until well browned. Remove the beef with a slotted spoon and set it aside.

2. Reduce the heat to medium and add the remaining oil. Add the carrots, onion, garlic and thyme. Cook and stir until the vegetables are tender-crisp.

3. Stir the soup, water, Worcestershire and black pepper into the skillet. Heat to a boil. Return the beef to the skillet and cook until the mixture is hot and bubbling. Serve over the noodles.

Prep Time: 10 minutes | **Cook Time:** 20 minutes

Herbed Beef & Vegetable Skillet

Perfect Potatoes

Roasted Potatoes and Pearl Onions

Makes 8 servings

3 pounds red potatoes, well-scrubbed and cut into 1½-inch cubes
1 package (10 ounces) pearl onions, peeled
2 tablespoons olive oil
2 teaspoons dried basil or thyme
1 teaspoon paprika
¾ teaspoon salt
¾ teaspoon dried rosemary
¾ teaspoon black pepper

1. Preheat oven to 400°F. Spray large shallow roasting pan (do not use glass baking dish or potatoes will not brown) with nonstick cooking spray.

2. Add potatoes and onions to pan; drizzle with oil. Combine basil, paprika, salt, rosemary and pepper in small bowl; mix well. Sprinkle over potatoes and onions; toss well to coat.

3. Bake 20 minutes; toss well. Continue baking 15 to 20 minutes or until potatoes are browned and tender.

Easy Cheesy Mashed Potatoes

Makes 8 servings, ½ cup each

WHAT YOU NEED

2 pounds Yukon gold potatoes (about 5), cubed
¼ cup milk
2 ounces VELVEETA® Pasteurized Prepared Cheese Product, cut into ½-inch cubes
¼ teaspoon garlic powder
1 green onion, thinly sliced

MAKE IT

1. COOK potatoes in large saucepan of boiling water 15 minutes or until tender. Drain potatoes; return to saucepan.

2. MASH potatoes until light and fluffy, gradually adding milk alternately with the VELVEETA®.

3. STIR in garlic powder. Top with onions.

Special Extra: For a change of pace, stir ¼ cup OSCAR MAYER® Real Bacon Bits into mashed potatoes with garlic powder.

Prep Time: 25 minutes | **Total Time:** 25 minutes

Easy Cheesy Mashed Potatoes

Potato, Beer and Cheese Gratin

Makes 8 servings

1 bottle (12 ounces) light-colored beer, such as pale ale
2 sprigs fresh thyme
1 bay leaf
½ cup whipping cream
1 tablespoon all-purpose flour
2 cloves garlic, minced
2 pounds potatoes (about 3 large), scrubbed and thinly sliced
1 teaspoon salt
1 teaspoon black pepper
2 cups (8 ounces) shredded Gruyère or Emmenthaler cheese
2 tablespoons chopped chives (optional)

1. Bring beer, thyme and bay leaf to a boil in medium saucepan over high heat. Reduce heat to medium. Cook and stir 5 minutes or until liquid reduces to ¾ cup. Remove and discard thyme and bay leaf. Let cool.

2. Combine cream, flour and garlic in small bowl; mix well. Stir into cooled beer mixture.

3. Preheat oven to 375°F. Grease 13×9-inch baking dish. Arrange half of potato slices in bottom of prepared dish, overlapping slightly. Sprinkle with salt and pepper. Pour half of cream-beer mixture over potatoes; sprinkle with half of cheese. Repeat layers.

4. Cover; bake gratin 30 minutes. *Reduce oven temperature to 350°F.* Uncover; bake 30 minutes or until potatoes are tender and top is golden brown. Let stand 10 minutes before serving. Garnish with chives.

Variation: Adding 1 teaspoon of minced jalapeño peppers to the gratin adds extra spice and balances the taste of the beer. Add the jalapeños with the cheese in step 3.

Potato, Beer and Cheese Gratin

Crispy Oven Fries with Herbed Dipping Sauce

Makes 3 servings

Herbed Dipping Sauce (recipe follows)
2 large baking potatoes
2 tablespoons vegetable oil
1 teaspoon kosher salt

1. Preheat oven to 425°F. Line two baking sheets with foil; spray with nonstick cooking spray. Prepare Herbed Dipping Sauce; set aside.

2. Cut potatoes lengthwise into ¼-inch slices, then cut each slice into ¼-inch strips. Place potato strips and oil in large bowl; toss well to coat. Arrange potato strips on baking sheets in single layer.

3. Bake 25 minutes; flip fries over. Bake additional 15 minutes or until light golden brown and crisp. Sprinkle with kosher salt. Serve immediately with dipping sauce.

Herbed Dipping Sauce: Combine ½ cup mayonnaise, 2 tablespoons chopped fresh herbs (such as basil, parsley, oregano or dill), 1 teaspoon salt and ½ teaspoon black pepper in small bowl.

Crispy Oven Fries with Herbed Dipping Sauce

Roasted Garlic Mashed Potatoes

Makes 6 to 8 servings

REYNOLDS WRAP® Aluminum Foil
2 large bulbs garlic
1 teaspoon olive oil
3 pounds large red potatoes, peeled and cubed
¼ cup milk, heated
¼ cup butter, softened
   Salt and black pepper
1 tablespoon chopped fresh parsley

Preheat oven to 400°F. Slice top of bulbs off unpeeled garlic. Remove papery outer layer of garlic bulbs. Place garlic on a sheet of REYNOLDS WRAP® Aluminum Foil. Drizzle with olive oil. Wrap in foil; place on a cookie sheet.

Bake 25 minutes or until garlic is soft. Cool. Squeeze pulp from garlic and mash in a bowl; set aside.

Place potatoes in large saucepan. Cook, covered, in boiling lightly salted water 20 to 25 minutes or until tender. Drain. Mash with potato masher or beat with electric mixer on low speed. Add roasted garlic, milk, butter, salt and pepper to taste. Beat until light and fluffy. Stir in parsley.

Prep Time: 15 minutes | **Cook Time:** 25 minutes

Roasted Garlic Mashed Potatoes

Buffalo Wedges
Makes 4 servings

3 pounds unpeeled Yukon Gold potatoes
3 tablespoons hot pepper sauce
2 tablespoons butter, melted
2 teaspoons smoked or sweet paprika
  Blue cheese dressing

1. Preheat oven to 400°F. Spray baking sheet with nonstick cooking spray. Cut each potato into 4 to 6 wedges, depending on size of potato.

2. Combine hot pepper sauce, butter and paprika in large bowl. Add potato wedges; toss to coat well. Place wedges in single layer on prepared baking sheet.

3. Bake 20 minutes. Turn potatoes; bake 20 minutes or until light golden brown and crisp. Serve with blue cheese dressing.

Heavenly Sweet Potatoes
Makes 8 servings

  Vegetable cooking spray
1 can (40 ounces) cut sweet potatoes in heavy syrup, drained
¼ teaspoon ground cinnamon
⅛ teaspoon ground ginger
¾ cup SWANSON® Chicken Broth (Regular, Natural Goodness® or Certified Organic)
2 cups miniature marshmallows

1. Heat the oven to 350°F.

2. Spray a 1½-quart casserole with cooking spray.

3. Put the potatoes, cinnamon and ginger in an electric mixer bowl. Beat at medium speed until almost smooth. Add the broth and beat until potatoes are fluffy. Spoon the potato mixture in the prepared dish. Top with the marshmallows.

4. Bake for 20 minutes or until heated through and marshmallows are golden brown.

Buffalo Wedges

Chunky Ranch Potatoes
Makes 8 servings

3 pounds unpeeled red potatoes, quartered
1 cup water
½ cup ranch dressing
½ cup grated Parmesan or Cheddar cheese
¼ cup minced chives

SLOW COOKER DIRECTIONS

1. Place potatoes and water in 4-quart slow cooker. Cover; cook on LOW 7 to 9 hours or on HIGH 4 to 6 hours or until potatoes are tender.

2. Stir in ranch dressing, cheese and chives. Break up potatoes into chunks.

Prep Time: 10 minutes | **Cook Time:** 7 to 9 hours (LOW) or 4 to 6 hours (HIGH)

Creamy Red Potato Salad
Makes 10 servings

3 pounds red bliss or new potatoes, cut into ¾-inch chunks
½ cup WISH-BONE® Italian Dressing*
¾ cup HELLMANN'S® or BEST FOODS® Real Mayonnaise
½ cup sliced green onions
1 teaspoon Dijon mustard
1 teaspoon lemon juice
⅛ teaspoon ground black pepper

*Also terrific with WISH-BONE® Robusto Italian or House Italian Dressing.

Cover potatoes with water in 4-quart saucepot; bring to a boil over medium-high heat. Reduce heat to low and simmer 10 minutes or until potatoes are tender. Drain and cool slightly.

Combine all ingredients except potatoes in large salad bowl. Add potatoes and toss gently. Serve chilled or at room temperature.

Prep Time: 15 minutes | **Cook Time:** 10 minutes

Chunky Ranch Potatoes

Double-Baked Potatoes

Makes 4 servings

2 large baking potatoes
1 tablespoon vegetable oil
2 teaspoons kosher salt, divided
½ cup (2 ounces) shredded sharp Cheddar cheese
¼ cup sour cream
2 tablespoons butter, softened
2 tablespoon chopped fresh chives, plus additional for garnish

1. Preheat oven to 350°F. Poke holes in potatoes using tines of fork. Rub potato skins with vegetable oil; sprinkle with 1 teaspoon salt. Bake potatoes 1 hour or until tender. Remove to wire rack; cool 10 minutes.

2. Cut potatoes in half lengthwise. Scoop potato pulp into medium bowl, leaving ½-inch shell. Add cheese, sour cream, butter, 2 tablespoons chives and remaining 1 teaspoon salt; mix well. Using piping bag fitted with large star tip, pipe potato mixture back into potato skins.

3. Place filled potato skins on baking sheet. Return to oven; bake 15 minutes or until light golden brown. Sprinkle with fresh chives.

Double-Baked Potatoes

Savory Herb Roasted Potatoes

Makes 4 to 6 servings

2 pounds red potatoes, cut into wedges (about 6 medium)
1⅓ cups *French's*® Cheddar French Fried Onions or *French's*® French Fried Onions
¼ cup parsley, minced
6 cloves garlic, halved
6 sprigs thyme or rosemary
2 tablespoons olive oil
1 teaspoon salt
¼ teaspoon ground black pepper
2 ice cubes
1 large foil oven roasting bag

1. Toss all ingredients in large bowl. Open foil bag; spoon potatoes into bag in an even layer. Seal bag with tight double folds. Place bag on baking sheet.

2. Place bag on grill over medium-high heat. Cover grill and cook 25 minutes until potatoes are tender, turning bag over once.

3. Return bag to baking sheet and carefully cut top of bag open. Sprinkle with additional French Fried Onions, if desired.

Note: Too cold for outdoor grilling? Bake these potatoes in a 450°F oven for 25 to 30 minutes.

Prep Time: 10 minutes | **Cook Time:** 25 minutes

Savory Herb Roasted Potatoes

Sweet Potato Fries

Makes 3 servings

1 teaspoon kosher salt
½ teaspoon black pepper
¼ teaspoon ground red pepper
2 large sweet potatoes, peeled
2 tablespoons vegetable oil

1. Preheat oven to 425°F. Line two baking sheets with foil; spray with cooking spray. Combine salt, black pepper and red pepper in small bowl; set aside.

2. Cut potatoes into long skinny spears. Place potato spears and oil in large bowl; toss well to coat. Arrange potatoes on baking sheets in single layer.

3. Bake 30 minutes or until lightly browned and crisp, turning potatoes once. Toss hot fries with seasoning mixture. Serve immediately.

Sweet Potato Fries

Taco-Topped Baked Potatoes
Makes 4 servings

4 large baking potatoes, scrubbed
½ pound (8 ounces) lean ground beef
¼ cup chopped onion
1 packet (1.25 ounces) ORTEGA® Taco Seasoning Mix
1 container (13 ounces) ORTEGA® Salsa & Cheese Bowl
Salt, to taste
Sour cream (optional)

PRICK potatoes several times with a fork. Microwave on HIGH, uncovered, 12 to 15 minutes or until just tender, turning potatoes over and re-arranging once.

CRUMBLE ground beef into 1-quart glass casserole; add onion. Microwave on HIGH, uncovered, 3 to 3½ minutes or until meat is heated through, stirring once; drain.

STIR in taco seasoning and half the amount of water specified on taco seasoning package. Add contents of Salsa & Cheese Bowl. Cover; microwave on HIGH (100%) 2½ to 3 minutes or until heated through, stirring once.

MAKE a crosswise slash in each potato; press side of potato to form an opening. Sprinkle with salt. Spoon filling into potatoes.

TOP each potato with sour cream, if desired.

Taco-Topped Baked Potato

Crispy Skillet Potatoes

Makes 4 servings

    2 tablespoons olive oil
    4 small red potatoes, cut into thin wedges
    ½ cup chopped onion
    2 tablespoons lemon pepper
    ½ teaspoon coarse salt
        Chopped fresh parsley

Heat oil in large skillet over medium heat. Add potatoes, onion, lemon pepper and salt; stir to combine. Cover and cook 25 to 30 minutes or until potatoes are tender and browned, turning occasionally. Sprinkle with parsley.

Tip: A cast iron skillet is the best way to cook crispy potatoes. Start the recipe on the stove and finish the last 15 minutes of cooking time in the oven at 400°F.

Crispy Skillet Potatoes

Donna's Potato Casserole

Makes 8 to 10 servings

1 can (10¾ ounces) condensed cream of chicken soup, undiluted
1 cup (8 ounces) sour cream
¼ cup chopped onion
¼ cup (½ stick) plus 3 tablespoons butter, melted, divided
1 teaspoon salt
2 pounds potatoes, peeled and chopped
2 cups (8 ounces) shredded Cheddar cheese
1½ to 2 cups stuffing mix

SLOW COOKER DIRECTIONS

1. Combine soup, sour cream, onion, ¼ cup butter and salt in small bowl.

2. Combine potatoes and cheese in slow cooker. Pour soup mixture over potato mixture; mix well. Sprinkle stuffing mix over potato mixture; drizzle with remaining 3 tablespoons butter.

3. Cover; cook on LOW 8 to 10 hours or on HIGH 5 to 6 hours or until potatoes are tender.

Prep Time: 10 minutes | **Cook Time:** 8 to 10 hours (LOW) or 5 to 6 hours (HIGH)

 Tip: Store raw potatoes in a cool, dark, dry, well-ventilated place. Do not refrigerate.

Casseroles

Table of Contents

Homestyle Meaty Meals

Ham, Poblano and Potato Casserole

Makes 6 servings

¼ cup (½ stick) butter
¼ cup all-purpose flour
1½ cups whole milk
 2 pounds baking potatoes, halved and thinly sliced
 6 ounces thinly sliced ham, cut into bite-size pieces
 1 poblano pepper, cut into thin strips (about 1 cup)
 1 cup corn
 1 cup chopped red bell pepper
 1 cup finely chopped onion
1½ teaspoons salt
 ¼ teaspoon black pepper
 ¼ teaspoon ground nutmeg
1½ cups (6 ounces) shredded sharp Cheddar cheese

1. Preheat oven to 350°F. Lightly coat 13×9-inch baking dish with nonstick cooking spray.

2. Melt butter in medium saucepan over medium heat. Add flour; whisk until smooth. Add milk; whisk until smooth. Cook and stir 5 to 7 minutes or until white sauce is thickened. Remove from heat.

3. Layer one third of potatoes, half of ham, poblano pepper, corn, bell pepper and onion in prepared baking dish. Sprinkle with half of salt, black pepper and nutmeg. Repeat layers. Top with remaining one third of potatoes. Spoon white sauce evenly over all.

4. Cover with foil; bake 45 minutes. Uncover; bake 30 minutes or until potatoes are tender. Sprinkle with cheese; bake 5 minutes or until melted. Let stand 15 minutes before serving.

Note: To make this casserole even easier, use a food processor with the slicing blade attachment to thinly slice potatoes.

Beef & Artichoke Casserole

Makes 4 servings

¾ **pound ground beef**
½ **cup sliced mushrooms**
¼ **cup chopped onion**
1 **clove garlic, minced**
1 **can (14 ounces) artichoke hearts, drained and chopped**
½ **cup dry bread crumbs**
¼ **cup (1 ounce) grated Parmesan cheese**
1 **tablespoon chopped fresh rosemary leaves** *or* **1 teaspoon dried rosemary**
1½ **teaspoons chopped fresh marjoram** *or* ½ **teaspoon dried marjoram**
Salt and black pepper
3 **egg whites**

1. Preheat oven to 400°F. Spray 1-quart casserole with nonstick cooking spray.

2. Brown ground beef in medium skillet 6 to 8 minutes over medium-high heat, stirring to break up meat. Drain fat. Add mushrooms, onion and garlic; cook and stir 5 minutes or until tender.

3. Combine ground beef mixture, artichokes, bread crumbs, cheese, rosemary and marjoram; mix lightly. Season with salt and pepper.

4. Beat egg whites in medium bowl with electric mixer at high speed until stiff peaks form; fold into ground beef mixture. Spoon into prepared casserole. Bake 20 minutes or until edges are lightly browned.

Beef & Artichoke Casserole

Layered Pasta Casserole

Makes 6 to 8 servings

8 ounces uncooked penne pasta
8 ounces mild Italian sausage, casings removed
8 ounces ground beef
1 jar (about 26 ounces) pasta sauce
1 package (10 ounces) frozen chopped spinach, thawed and
    squeezed dry
2 cups (8 ounces) shredded mozzarella cheese, divided
1 cup ricotta cheese
½ cup grated Parmesan cheese
1 egg
2 tablespoons chopped fresh basil *or* 2 teaspoons dried basil
1 teaspoon salt

1. Preheat oven to 350°F. Spray 13×9-inch baking dish with nonstick cooking spray. Cook pasta according to package directions; drain. Transfer to prepared dish.

2. Brown sausage and beef 6 to 8 minutes in large skillet over medium-high heat, stirring to break up meat. Drain fat. Add pasta sauce; mix well. Add half of meat sauce to pasta; toss to coat.

3. Combine spinach, 1 cup mozzarella, ricotta, Parmesan, egg, basil and salt in medium bowl. Spoon small mounds of spinach mixture over pasta mixture; spread evenly with back of spoon. Top with remaining meat sauce; sprinkle with remaining 1 cup mozzarella. Bake 30 minutes or until heated through.

Layered Pasta Casserole

Wisconsin Swiss Ham and Noodles Casserole

Makes 6 to 8 servings

2 tablespoons butter
½ cup chopped onion
½ cup chopped green bell pepper
1 can (10½ ounces) condensed cream of mushroom soup
1 cup dairy sour cream
1 package (8 ounces) medium noodles, cooked and drained
2 cups (8 ounces) shredded Wisconsin Swiss cheese
2 cups cubed cooked ham (about ¾ pound)

In 1-quart saucepan, melt butter; sauté onion and bell pepper. Remove from heat; stir in soup and sour cream. In buttered 2-quart casserole, layer ⅓ of the noodles, ⅓ of the Swiss cheese, ⅓ of the ham and ½ soup mixture. Repeat layers, ending with final ⅓ layer of noodles, cheese and ham. Bake in preheated 350°F oven 30 to 45 minutes or until heated through.

Favorite recipe from *Wisconsin Milk Marketing Board*

Wisconsin Swiss Ham and Noodles Casserole

Tuscan Vegetable and Sausage Casserole

Makes 8 servings, about 1¼ cups each

WHAT YOU NEED

4 cups penne pasta, cooked, drained
1 pound Italian sausage, cut into ½-inch-thick slices
1 package (16 ounces) frozen Italian-style vegetable combination
½ pound (8 ounces) VELVEETA® 2% Milk Pasteurized Prepared Cheese
     Product, cut into ½-inch cubes
1 jar (14 ounces) spaghetti sauce
⅓ cup milk
⅓ cup KRAFT® Grated Parmesan Cheese

MAKE IT

1. HEAT oven to 400°F. Combine all ingredients except Parmesan in 13×9-inch baking dish; cover with foil.

2. BAKE 40 minutes or until sausage is done and casserole is heated through; stir.

3. Top with Parmesan.

Great Leftovers: Refrigerate any leftovers. To reheat, spoon 1⅓ cups pasta mixture onto microwaveable plate; cover with paper towel. Microwave on HIGH 2 to 2½ minutes or until heated through. Repeat for additional servings as needed.

Prep Time: 25 minutes | Total Time: 1 hour 10 minutes

Tuscan Vegetable and Sausage Casserole

Cajun-Style Beef and Beans
Makes 6 servings

  1 pound ground beef
  ¾ cup chopped onion
2½ cups cooked brown rice
  1 can (about 15 ounces) kidney beans, rinsed and drained
  1 can (about 14 ounces) stewed tomatoes
  2 teaspoons Cajun seasoning, or to taste
  ¾ cup (3 ounces) shredded Cheddar cheese

1. Preheat oven to 350°F. Brown beef in large nonstick skillet 6 to 8 minutes over medium-high heat, stirring to break up meat. Drain fat. Add onion; cook and stir 2 minutes or until translucent.

2. Combine beef mixture, rice, beans, tomatoes and Cajun seasoning in 2- to 2½-quart casserole. Cover; bake 25 to 30 minutes, stirring once. Sprinkle with cheese. Cover and let stand 5 minutes before serving.

Prep Time: 35 minutes | **Bake Time:** 25 to 30 minutes
Stand Time: 5 minutes

Tip: To make Cajun seasoning, combine 5 tablespoons ground red pepper, 3 tablespoons black pepper, 3 tablespoons onion powder, 3 tablespoons garlic powder, 3 tablespoons chili powder, 1 tablespoon dried thyme, 1 tablespoon dried basil and 1 tablespoon ground bay leaf in a medium bowl until the spices are well combined. Stir in ½ cup salt, if desired. Store in a tightly sealed container at room temperature.

Cajun-Style Beef and Beans

Baked Ziti

Makes 8 servings

REYNOLDS WRAP® Non-Stick Foil
1 pound ground beef, browned and drained
4 cups (32-ounce jar) chunky garden-style pasta sauce
1 tablespoon Italian seasoning, divided
1 package (16 ounces) ziti pasta, cooked and drained
1 package (8 ounces) shredded mozzarella cheese, divided
1 container (16 ounces) ricotta cheese or cottage cheese
1 egg
¼ cup grated Parmesan cheese, divided

Preheat oven to 350°F.

Combine ground beef, pasta sauce and 2 teaspoons Italian seasoning. Stir pasta into meat sauce; spread half of mixture evenly in 13×9-inch baking pan. Top with half of mozzarella cheese.

Combine ricotta cheese, egg, 2 tablespoons Parmesan cheese and remaining Italian seasoning; spread over mozzarella cheese in pan. Spread remaining pasta mixture over ricotta cheese mixture. Sprinkle with remaining mozzarella and Parmesan cheeses.

Cover with Reynolds Wrap Non-Stick Foil with non-stick (dull) side toward food.

Bake 45 minutes. Remove foil and continue baking 15 minutes or until cheese is melted and lightly browned. Let stand 15 minutes before serving.

Prep Time: 20 minutes | **Cook Time:** 1 hour

Baked Ziti

Pork and Corn Bread Stuffing Casserole

Makes 4 servings

½ teaspoon paprika
¼ teaspoon salt
¼ teaspoon garlic powder
¼ teaspoon black pepper
4 bone-in pork chops (about 1¾ pounds)
2 tablespoons butter
1½ cups chopped onions
¾ cup thinly sliced celery
¾ cup matchstick or shredded carrots
¼ cup chopped fresh Italian parsley
1 can (about 14 ounces) chicken broth
4 cups corn bread stuffing mix

1. Preheat oven to 350°F. Lightly coat 13×9-inch baking dish with nonstick cooking spray.

2. Combine paprika, salt, garlic powder and pepper in small bowl. Sprinkle over both sides of pork chops.

3. Melt butter in large skillet over medium-high heat. Add pork chops; cook 4 minutes or just until browned, turning once. Transfer to plate.

4. Add onions, celery, carrots and parsley to same skillet; cook and stir 4 minutes or until onions are translucent. Add broth; bring to a boil. Remove from heat; add stuffing mix and fluff with fork.

5. Transfer stuffing mixture to prepared baking dish. Top with pork chops. Cover; bake 25 minutes or until pork is barely pink in center.

Variation: For a one-dish meal, use an ovenproof skillet. Place browned pork chops on mixture in skillet; cover and bake as directed.

Pork and Corn Bread Stuffing Casserole

Taco Pot Pie

Makes 4 to 6 servings

1 pound ground beef
1 package (1¼ ounces) taco seasoning mix
¼ cup water
1 cup canned kidney beans, rinsed and drained
1 cup chopped tomato
¾ cup frozen corn, thawed
¾ cup frozen peas, thawed
1½ cups (6 ounces) shredded Cheddar cheese
1 can (11½ ounces) refrigerated breadstick dough

1. Preheat oven to 400°F. Brown beef in medium ovenproof skillet 6 to 8 minutes over medium-high heat, stirring to break up meat. Drain fat. Add taco seasoning mix and water to skillet. Cook and stir over medium-low heat 3 minutes or until most liquid is absorbed.

2. Stir in beans, tomato, corn and peas. Cook 3 minutes or until mixture is heated through. Remove from heat; stir in cheese.

3. Unwrap breadstick dough; separate into strips. Twist strips, cutting to fit skillet. Arrange attractively over meat mixture. Press ends of dough lightly to edge of skillet to secure. Bake 15 minutes or until bread is golden brown and meat mixture is bubbly.

Prep and Cook Time: **30 minutes**

Taco Pot Pie

Creamy Beef, Carrot and Noodle Baked Stroganoff

Makes 6 servings

1 pound ground beef
1 large onion, diced (about 1 cup)
2 cans (10¾ ounces each) CAMPBELL'S® Condensed Cream of
   Mushroom Soup (Regular or 98% Fat Free)
2 cups water
2 cups frozen crinkle-cut carrots, thawed
2 cups uncooked medium egg noodles
½ cup sour cream

1. Cook the beef and onion in a 12-inch skillet until the beef is well browned, stirring frequently to separate meat. Pour off any fat. Spoon the beef mixture into a 13×9×2-inch (3-quart) shallow baking dish. Stir the soup, water, carrots, noodles and sour cream into the dish. Cover.

2. Bake at 375°F. for 30 minutes or until hot and bubbly.

Prep Time: **10 minutes** | Bake Time: **30 minutes**

Creamy Beef, Carrot and Noodle Baked Stroganoff

Easy Lasagna
Makes 8 to 10 servings

1 pound ground beef
1 jar (26 ounces) pasta sauce
1 container (16 ounces) small curd cottage cheese
8 ounces sour cream
8 uncooked lasagna noodles
3 packages (6 ounces each) sliced mozzarella cheese (12 slices)
½ cup grated Parmesan cheese
1 cup water

1. Brown beef in large skillet 6 to 8 minutes over medium-high heat, stirring to break up meat. Drain fat. Add pasta sauce. Reduce heat to low; cook and stir until heated through.

2. Preheat oven to 350°F.

3. Combine cottage cheese and sour cream in medium bowl; blend well.

4. Spoon 1½ cups meat sauce into 13×9-inch baking dish. Layer with 4 uncooked noodles, half of cottage cheese mixture, 4 slices mozzarella, half of remaining meat sauce and ¼ cup Parmesan. Repeat layers starting with noodles. Top with remaining 4 slices mozzarella. Pour water into dish around sides. Cover tightly with foil.

5. Bake 1 hour. Uncover; bake 20 minutes more or until bubbly. Let stand 15 to 20 minutes before cutting.

Easy Lasagna

Biscuit-Topped Hearty Steak Pie

Makes 6 servings

1½ pounds top round steak, cooked and cut into 1-inch cubes
1 package (9 ounces) frozen baby carrots
1 package (9 ounces) frozen peas and pearl onions
1 large baking potato, cut into ½-inch pieces
1 jar (18 ounces) homestyle brown gravy
½ teaspoon dried thyme
½ teaspoon black pepper
1 can (10 ounces) refrigerated flaky buttermilk biscuit dough

1. Preheat oven to 375°F. Spray 2-quart casserole with nonstick cooking spray.

2. Combine steak, carrots, peas, potato, gravy, thyme and pepper in large bowl. Pour into prepared casserole.

3. Bake 40 minutes. Remove from oven. *Increase oven temperature to 400°F.* Top with biscuits and bake 8 to 10 minutes or until biscuits are golden brown.

Variations: This casserole can be prepared with leftovers of almost any kind. Roast beef, stew meat, pork, lamb or chicken can be substituted for the round steak. Adjust the gravy flavor to complement the meat. Choose your favorite vegetable combination as a substitute for the carrots, peas and onions.

Biscuit-Topped Hearty Steak Pie

Oven Pork Cassoulet

Makes 6 servings

1 tablespoon canola oil
1¼ pounds pork tenderloin, cut into 1-inch pieces
1 cup chopped onion
1 cup chopped carrots
3 cloves garlic, minced
2 cans (about 15 ounces each) cannellini beans, rinsed and drained
1 can (about 14 ounces) diced tomatoes with Italian seasoning
¼ pound smoked turkey sausage, cut into ¼-inch-thick slices
1 teaspoon dried thyme
¼ teaspoon salt
¼ teaspoon dried rosemary
¼ teaspoon black pepper

1. Preheat oven to 325°F. Heat oil in Dutch oven over medium heat; brown pork in batches. Transfer pork to plate.

2. Add onion, carrots and garlic to Dutch oven; cook and stir 8 to 10 minutes or until tender.

3. Combine pork, onion mixture and remaining ingredients in 3-quart casserole. Cover; bake 35 to 40 minutes or until heated through.

Prep Time: 15 minutes | Bake Time: 35 to 40 minutes

Oven Pork Cassoulet

Hearty Beef and Potato Casserole

Makes 6 servings

1 package (about 17 ounces) refrigerated fully cooked beef pot roast in gravy*
3 cups frozen hash brown potatoes, divided
¼ teaspoon salt
¼ teaspoon black pepper
1 can (about 14 ounces) diced tomatoes
½ cup canned chipotle chile sauce
1 cup (4 ounces) shredded sharp Cheddar cheese

Fully cooked beef pot roast in gravy can be found in the refrigerated prepared meats section of the supermarket.

1. Preheat oven to 375°F. Lightly coat 11×7-inch baking dish with nonstick cooking spray.

2. Drain and discard gravy from pot roast. Cut beef into ¼-inch-thick slices. Place 2 cups potatoes in prepared baking dish. Sprinkle with salt and pepper. Top with beef. Combine tomatoes and chile sauce in small bowl; spread evenly over beef. Top with remaining 1 cup potatoes. Sprinkle with cheese.

3. Cover; bake 20 minutes. Uncover; bake 20 minutes or until heated through. Let stand 5 minutes before serving.

Hearty Beef and Potato Casserole

Fish & Poultry

Turkey Pot Pie Casserole

Makes 6 servings

Nonstick cooking spray
2 pounds turkey breast, cut into 1-inch cubes
6 tablespoons butter
⅓ cup all-purpose flour
½ teaspoon ground sage
½ teaspoon ground thyme
1½ cups chicken broth
1 cup milk
1 bag (16 ounces) frozen soup vegetables, thawed
1 teaspoon salt
½ teaspoon black pepper
1 container (8 ounces) refrigerated crescent roll dough

1. Preheat oven to 375°F. Coat 13×9-inch baking dish with cooking spray.

2. Coat large nonstick skillet with cooking spray; heat over medium heat. Brown turkey on all sides in batches. Transfer to platter.

3. Melt butter in same skillet. Whisk in flour, sage and thyme; cook and stir 5 minutes. Slowly whisk in broth and milk; cook, whisking constantly, about 5 minutes or until thickened.

4. Add turkey, vegetables, salt and pepper; cook and stir 5 to 7 minutes or until thick and creamy. Spoon mixture into prepared baking dish. Unroll crescent roll dough. Place over top of casserole. Bake 15 minutes or until golden brown.

Tuna-Macaroni Casserole

Makes 6 servings

1 cup mayonnaise
1 cup (4 ounces) shredded Swiss cheese
½ cup milk
¼ cup chopped onion
¼ cup chopped red bell pepper
⅛ teaspoon black pepper
2 cans (7 ounces each) tuna, drained and flaked
1 package (about 10 ounces) frozen peas
2 cups uncooked shell pasta or elbow macaroni, cooked and drained
½ cup dry bread crumbs
2 tablespoons melted butter
Chopped fresh parsley (optional)

1. Preheat oven to 350°F.

2. Combine mayonnaise, cheese, milk, onion, bell pepper and black pepper in large bowl. Add tuna, peas and macaroni; toss to coat well. Spoon into 2-quart casserole.

3. Mix bread crumbs with butter in small bowl and sprinkle over top of casserole. Bake 30 to 40 minutes or until heated through. Garnish with chopped parsley.

Tuna-Macaroni Casserole

Turkey Veggie Tetrazzini

Makes 12 servings

8 ounces dry whole wheat spaghetti
1 package (16 ounces) frozen Italian-style vegetable blend
    (broccoli, red peppers, mushrooms and onions)
1 tablespoon olive oil
¼ cup all-purpose flour
½ teaspoon garlic powder
¼ teaspoon salt
¼ teaspoon ground black pepper
1 can (14.5 fluid ounces) reduced sodium chicken broth
1 can (12 fluid ounces) NESTLÉ® CARNATION® Evaporated
    Lowfat 2% Milk
¾ cup (2.25 ounces) shredded Parmesan cheese, *divided*
2 cups cooked, chopped turkey breast meat

PREHEAT oven to 350°F. Lightly grease 13×9-inch baking dish.

PREPARE pasta according to package directions, adding frozen vegetables to boiling pasta water for last minute of cooking time; drain. Return pasta and vegetables to cooking pot.

MEANWHILE, HEAT oil in medium saucepan over medium heat. Stir in flour, garlic powder, salt and pepper; cook, stirring constantly, for 1 minute. Remove from heat; gradually stir in broth. Return to heat; bring to boil, stirring constantly. Stir in evaporated milk and *½ cup* cheese; cook over low heat until cheese melts. Remove from heat. Stir in turkey.

POUR cheese sauce over pasta and vegetables; mix lightly. Pour into prepared baking dish. Sprinkle with *remaining ¼ cup* cheese.

BAKE for 20 to 25 minutes or until lightly browned. Serve immediately.

Turkey Veggie Tetrazzini

Seafood Pasta

Makes 6 servings

½ cup olive oil
1 pound asparagus, trimmed and cut into 1-inch pieces
1 cup chopped green onions
5 teaspoons chopped garlic
1 package (about 16 ounces) linguine, cooked and drained
1 pound medium cooked shrimp, shelled and deveined
1 package (8 ounces) imitation crabmeat, roughly chopped
1 package (8 ounces) imitation lobster, roughly chopped
1 can (8 ounces) sliced black olives, drained

1. Preheat oven to 350°F. Spray 4-quart casserole with nonstick cooking spray.

2. Heat oil in large skillet over medium heat. Add asparagus, green onions and garlic; cook and stir until tender.

3. Combine asparagus mixture, linguine, seafood and olives in prepared casserole. Bake 30 minutes or until heated through.

Seafood Pasta

Chili Cornbread Pie

Makes 10 to 12 servings

1 pound ground turkey or lean ground beef
1 packet (1.4 ounces) chili seasoning or taco seasoning mix
2 cans (8 ounces *each*) tomato sauce
1 can (15¼ ounces) no-salt added whole-kernel corn, drained
1 can (15 ounces) black beans, rinsed and drained
1 can (12 fluid ounces) NESTLÉ® CARNATION® Evaporated Milk,
    divided
1 can (4 ounces) diced green chilies, drained (optional)
2 boxes (8.5 ounces *each*) dry corn muffin mix
2 eggs, beaten
    Sliced avocado, salsa and/or sour cream (optional)

PREHEAT oven to 400°F. Grease 13×9-inch baking dish.

COOK turkey in large skillet over medium-high heat until turkey is no longer pink; drain. Stir in chili seasoning, tomato sauce, corn, beans, ¾ *cup* evaporated milk and chilies. Bring to a boil, reduce heat. Simmer for 5 minutes, stirring occasionally. Pour mixture into prepared baking dish.

COMBINE corn muffin mix, *remaining* ¾ *cup* evaporated milk and eggs in medium bowl; stir until just moistened. Spread mixture over meat filling.

BAKE for 15 to 20 minutes or until lightly browned. Let stand for 10 minutes before serving.

Serving Suggestion: Serve with chopped avocado, sour cream and salsa.

Chili Cornbread Pie

Company Crab
Makes 6 servings

1 pound Florida blue crabmeat, fresh, frozen or pasteurized
1 can (15 ounces) artichoke hearts, drained
1 can (4 ounces) sliced mushrooms, drained
2 tablespoons butter or margarine
2½ tablespoons all-purpose flour
½ teaspoon salt
⅛ teaspoon ground red pepper
1 cup half-and-half
2 tablespoons dry sherry
2 tablespoons crushed cornflakes
1 tablespoon grated Parmesan cheese
Paprika

Preheat oven to 450°F. Thaw crabmeat if frozen. Remove any pieces of shell or cartilage. Cut artichoke hearts in half; place artichokes in well-greased, shallow 1½-quart casserole. Add crabmeat and mushrooms; cover and set aside.

Melt butter in small saucepan over medium heat. Stir in flour, salt and ground red pepper. Gradually stir in half-and-half. Continue cooking until sauce thickens, stirring constantly. Stir in sherry. Pour sauce over crabmeat. Combine cornflakes and cheese in small bowl; sprinkle over casserole. Sprinkle with paprika. Bake 12 to 15 minutes or until bubbly.

Favorite recipe from *Florida Department of Agriculture and Consumer Services, Bureau of Seafood and Aquaculture*

Company Crab

Chicken & Biscuits

Makes 4 to 6 servings

¼ cup (½ stick) butter or margarine
4 boneless skinless chicken breasts (about 1¼ pounds), cut into
     ½-inch pieces
½ cup chopped onion
½ teaspoon dried thyme
½ teaspoon paprika
¼ teaspoon black pepper
1 can (about 14 ounces) chicken broth, divided
⅓ cup all-purpose flour
1 package (10 ounces) frozen peas and carrots
1 can (12 ounces) refrigerated biscuit dough

1. Preheat oven to 375°F. Melt butter in large skillet over medium heat. Add chicken, onion, thyme, paprika and pepper. Cook 5 minutes or until chicken is browned.

2. Combine ¼ cup chicken broth with flour in small bowl; stir until smooth. Set aside.

3. Add remaining chicken broth to skillet; bring to a boil. Gradually add flour mixture, whisking constantly to prevent lumps from forming. Simmer 5 minutes. Add peas and carrots; cook 2 minutes.

4. Transfer mixture to 1½-quart casserole; top with biscuits. Bake 25 to 30 minutes or until biscuits are golden brown.

Tip: Cook the chicken in an ovenproof skillet instead of the 1½-quart casserole. Place the biscuits directly on the chicken and vegetable mixture, then bake as directed.

Chicken & Biscuits

Shrimp and Chicken Paella

Makes 4 servings

¾ cup cooked rice
2 cans (about 14 ounces each) diced tomatoes
½ teaspoon ground turmeric *or* ⅛ teaspoon saffron threads
1 package (¾ pound) frozen medium shrimp, thawed, peeled and deveined (about 3 cups)
2 chicken tenders (about 4 ounces), cut into 1-inch pieces
1 cup frozen peas

1. Preheat oven to 400°F. Lightly coat 8-inch glass baking dish with nonstick cooking spray. Spread rice in prepared dish.

2. Pour 1 can of tomatoes with juice over rice; sprinkle turmeric over tomatoes. Arrange shrimp and chicken over tomatoes. Top with peas.

3. Drain remaining can of tomatoes, discarding juice. Spread tomatoes evenly over shrimp and chicken. Cover; bake 30 minutes. Let stand, covered, 5 minutes before serving.

Serving Suggestion: Serve with a green salad tossed with mustard vinaigrette and garnished with ½ cup corn kernels.

Shrimp and Chicken Paella

Country Chicken Pot Pie

Makes 6 servings

2 tablespoons butter
1 pound boneless skinless chicken breasts, cut into 1-inch pieces
¾ teaspoon salt
8 ounces fresh green beans, cut into 1-inch pieces (2 cups)
½ cup chopped red bell pepper
½ cup thinly sliced celery
3 tablespoons all-purpose flour
½ cup chicken broth
½ cup half-and-half
1 teaspoon dried thyme
½ teaspoon dried sage
1 cup frozen pearl onions
½ cup frozen corn
Pastry for single-crust 10-inch pie

1. Preheat oven to 425°F. Spray 10-inch deep-dish pie plate with nonstick cooking spray.

2. Melt butter in large deep skillet over medium-high heat. Add chicken; cook and stir 3 minutes or until no longer pink in center. Sprinkle with salt. Add beans, bell pepper and celery; cook and stir 3 minutes.

3. Sprinkle flour evenly over chicken and vegetables; cook and stir 1 minute. Stir in broth, half-and-half, thyme and sage; bring to a boil over high heat. Reduce heat to low and simmer 3 minutes or until sauce is very thick. Stir in onions and corn. Return to a simmer; cook and stir 1 minute.

4. Transfer mixture to prepared pie plate. Place pie crust over chicken mixture; turn edge under and crimp to seal. Cut 4 slits or decorative pieces out of pie crust to allow steam to escape. Bake 20 minutes or until crust is light golden brown and mixture is hot and bubbly. Let stand 5 minutes before serving.

Serving Suggestion: Serve with chunky applesauce.

Country Chicken Pot Pie

Velveeta® Tuna Noodle Casserole

Makes 8 servings, about 1 cup each

WHAT YOU NEED

4 cups egg noodles, cooked, drained
1 package (16 ounces) frozen peas and carrots
2 cans (6 ounces each) tuna, drained, flaked
1 can (10¾ ounces) condensed cream of mushroom soup
⅓ cup milk
¾ pound (12 ounces) VELVEETA® Pasteurized Prepared Cheese
     Product, cut into ½-inch cubes
1 can (2.8 ounces) French fried onion rings

MAKE IT

1. HEAT oven to 400°F. Combine all ingredients except onions in 13×9-inch baking dish; cover with foil.

2. BAKE 45 minutes or until heated through; stir.

3. TOP with onions.

Variation: Prepare using reduced-fat condensed cream of mushroom soup and VELVEETA® 2% Milk Pasteurized Prepared Cheese Product.

Prep Time: 20 minutes | Total Time: 55 minutes

Velveeta® Tuna Noodle Casserole

Chipotle Turkey Strata
Makes 6 servings

6 to 8 (½-inch-thick) Italian bread slices
2 tablespoons chipotle sauce*
2 cups chopped cooked dark turkey meat
1½ cups (6 ounces) shredded Cheddar cheese, divided**
5 eggs
2½ cups milk
½ teaspoon salt
¼ teaspoon black pepper

If you can't find chipotle sauce, substitute 1 tablespoon tomato sauce mixed with 1 tablespoon adobo sauce with chipotles.

**For a spicier dish, substitute Monterey Jack cheese with jalapeño peppers.*

1. Preheat oven to 325°F. Grease 9-inch square baking pan.

2. Arrange 3 to 4 bread slices to cover bottom of pan. Cut bread to fit, if necessary. Spread chipotle sauce over bread. Arrange turkey over sauce. Sprinkle 1 cup cheese over turkey. Cover with remaining 3 to 4 bread slices.

3. Beat eggs, milk, salt and pepper in medium bowl. Pour over bread; press down firmly so bread absorbs liquid. Top with remaining ½ cup cheese.

4. Bake 60 to 70 minutes or until golden brown. Remove from oven. Let stand 10 to 15 minutes before cutting.

Tip: This dish can be assembled up to 8 hours in advance. Cover with foil and refrigerate until needed. Bake as directed.

Chipotle Turkey Strata

Louisiana Seafood Bake

Makes 4 servings

1 can (14½ ounces) whole tomatoes, undrained and cut up
1 can (8 ounces) tomato sauce
1 cup water
1 cup sliced celery
⅔ cup uncooked regular rice
1⅓ cups *French's*® French Fried Onions, divided
1 teaspoon *Frank's*® *RedHot*® Original Cayenne Pepper Sauce
½ teaspoon garlic powder
¼ teaspoon dried oregano, crumbled
¼ teaspoon dried thyme, crumbled
½ pound white fish, thawed if frozen and cut into 1-inch chunks
1 can (4 ounces) shrimp, drained
⅓ cup sliced pitted ripe olives
¼ cup (1 ounce) grated Parmesan cheese

Preheat oven to 375°F. In 1½-quart casserole, combine tomatoes, tomato sauce, water, celery, uncooked rice, ⅔ *cup* French Fried Onions and seasonings. Bake, covered, at 375°F for 20 minutes. Stir in fish, shrimp and olives. Bake, covered, 20 minutes or until heated through. Top with cheese and remaining ⅔ *cup* onions; bake, uncovered, 3 minutes or until onions are golden brown.

Microwave Directions: In 2-quart microwave-safe casserole, prepare rice mixture as above. Cook, covered, on HIGH 15 minutes, stirring rice halfway through cooking time. Add fish, shrimp and olives. Cook, covered, 12 to 14 minutes or until rice is cooked. Stir casserole halfway through cooking time. Top with cheese and remaining ⅔ cup onions; cook, uncovered, 1 minute. Let stand 5 minutes.

Louisiana Seafood Bake

Salmon Casserole

Makes 8 servings

2 tablespoons butter or vegetable oil
2 cups sliced mushrooms
1½ cups chopped carrots
1 cup frozen peas
1 cup chopped celery
½ cup chopped onion
½ cup chopped red bell pepper
1 tablespoon chopped fresh Italian parsley
1 clove garlic, minced
1 teaspoon salt
½ teaspoon black pepper
½ teaspoon dried basil
4 cups cooked rice
1 can (about 14 ounces) red salmon, drained and flaked
1 can (10¾ ounces) condensed cream of mushroom soup, undiluted
2 cups (8 ounces) shredded Cheddar or American cheese
½ cup sliced black olives

1. Preheat oven to 350°F. Lightly coat 2-quart casserole with nonstick cooking spray.

2. Melt butter in large saucepan or Dutch oven over medium heat. Add mushrooms, carrots, peas, celery, onion, bell pepper, parsley, garlic, salt, black pepper and basil; cook and stir 10 minutes or until vegetables are tender. Add rice, salmon, soup and cheese; mix well.

3. Transfer to prepared casserole; sprinkle with olives. Bake 30 minutes or until hot and bubbly.

Salmon Casserole

Chicken Divan Casserole

Makes 6 servings

Nonstick cooking spray
1 cup uncooked rice
1 cup coarsely shredded carrots
4 boneless skinless chicken breasts
2 tablespoons butter
3 tablespoons all-purpose flour
¼ teaspoon salt
Black pepper
1 cup chicken broth
½ cup milk or half-and-half
¼ cup dry white wine
⅓ cup plus 2 tablespoons grated Parmesan cheese, divided
1 pound frozen broccoli florets

1. Preheat oven to 350°F. Spray 12×8-inch baking dish with cooking spray.

2. Prepare rice according to package directions. Stir in carrots. Spread mixture in prepared baking dish.

3. Spray large skillet with cooking spray; heat over medium-high heat. Brown chicken about 2 minutes on each side. Arrange over rice.

4. Melt butter in medium saucepan over medium heat. Whisk in flour, salt and pepper; cook and stir 1 minute. Gradually whisk in broth and milk. Cook and stir until mixture comes to a boil. Reduce heat; simmer 2 minutes. Stir in wine. Remove from heat. Stir in ⅓ cup cheese.

5. Arrange broccoli around chicken. Pour sauce over top. Sprinkle remaining 2 tablespoons cheese over chicken.

6. Cover with foil; bake 30 minutes. Remove foil; bake 10 to 15 minutes or until chicken is no longer pink in center.

Chicken Divan Casserole

Meatless Mains

Garlic Spinach Lasagna
Makes 8 servings

12 uncooked lasagna noodles
2 tablespoons olive oil
4 cloves garlic, chopped
2 cups frozen chopped spinach, thawed and squeezed dry
   Salt and black pepper
3 cups ricotta cheese
¾ cup plus 2 tablespoons grated Parmesan cheese, divided
2 eggs, lightly beaten
1 jar (about 24 ounces) pasta sauce
2 cups (8 ounces) shredded provolone or mozzarella cheese

1. Cook lasagna noodles according to package directions. Drain; cover and keep warm. Preheat oven to 350°F.

2. Heat oil in medium nonstick skillet over medium heat. Add garlic; cook and stir 30 seconds. Add spinach, salt and pepper; cook and stir 3 minutes.

3. Combine ricotta, ¾ cup Parmesan and eggs in medium bowl; mix well.

4. Spread 3 tablespoons pasta sauce in bottom of 13×9-inch baking dish. Layer 4 noodles,1 cup sauce, half of ricotta mixture, half of spinach mixture and ½ cup provolone in dish. Repeat layers. Top with remaining noodles, sauce, 1 cup provolone and 2 tablespoons Parmesan.

5. Cover tightly with foil. Bake 30 minutes or until hot and bubbly. Remove foil; bake 15 minutes or until browned.

Cauliflower Mac & Gouda

Makes 6 to 8 servings

1 package (about 16 ounces) bowtie pasta
4 cups milk
2 cloves garlic, peeled and smashed
¼ cup (½ stick) plus 3 tablespoons butter, divided
5 tablespoons all-purpose flour
1 pound Gouda cheese, shredded
1 teaspoon dry mustard
⅛ teaspoon smoked paprika or paprika
   Salt and black pepper
1 head cauliflower, cored and cut into florets
1 cup panko bread crumbs

1. Cook pasta according to package directions until almost tender. Drain pasta, reserving pasta water; keep warm. Return water to a boil.

2. Bring milk and garlic to a boil in small saucepan. Reduce heat; keep warm. Discard garlic.

3. Melt ¼ cup butter in large saucepan over medium heat; whisk in flour. Cook 1 minute, whisking constantly. Gradually add milk, whisking after each addition. Bring to a boil. Reduce heat; cook and stir 10 minutes or until thickened. Remove from heat.

4. Add cheese, mustard and paprika to sauce mixture; whisk until melted. Season with salt and pepper. Keep warm.

5. Preheat broiler. Add cauliflower to boiling pasta water. Cook 3 to 5 minutes or just until tender; drain. Toss pasta and cauliflower with sauce mixture. Spoon pasta mixture into ramekins or 13×9-inch baking dish.

6. Melt remaining 3 tablespoons butter in small saucepan over medium heat. Add panko; stir just until moistened. Remove from heat. Sprinkle panko mixture over pasta mixture. Broil 2 minutes or until golden brown.

Cauliflower Mac & Gouda

Southwestern Corn and Pasta Casserole

Makes 4 servings

2 tablespoons vegetable oil
1 onion, chopped
1 red bell pepper, chopped
1 jalapeño pepper,* minced
1 clove garlic, minced
1 cup sliced mushrooms
2 cups frozen corn, thawed
½ teaspoon salt
¼ teaspoon ground cumin
¼ teaspoon chili powder
4 ounces whole wheat elbow macaroni, cooked and drained
1½ cups milk
1 tablespoon unsalted butter
1 tablespoon all-purpose flour
1 cup (4 ounces) shredded Monterey Jack cheese with chiles
1 slice whole wheat bread, cut or torn into ½-inch pieces

Jalapeño peppers can sting and irritate the skin, so wear rubber gloves when handling peppers and do not touch your eyes.

1. Preheat oven to 350°F. Grease 3-quart glass baking dish.

2. Heat oil in large skillet over medium-high heat. Add onion, bell pepper, jalapeño and garlic; cook and stir 5 minutes. Add mushrooms; cook 5 minutes longer. Add corn, salt, cumin and chili powder. Reduce heat; stir in corn and macaroni. Set aside.

3. Heat milk in small saucepan until simmering. Melt butter in large saucepan. Stir in flour to make a paste. Gradually whisk in milk; cook and stir over medium-low heat 5 to 7 minutes or until slightly thickened. Gradually stir in cheese; remove from heat. Stir macaroni mixture into cheese sauce; mix well.

4. Spoon into prepared baking dish. Sprinkle bread pieces over casserole. Bake 20 to 25 minutes or until bubbly. Let stand 5 minutes before serving.

Southwestern Corn and Pasta Casserole

Caramelized Onion Tart

Makes 6 to 8 servings

2 tablespoons butter
4 cups sliced onions
½ teaspoon salt
½ teaspoon dried thyme
½ cup ORTEGA® Salsa
2 tablespoons ORTEGA® Diced Jalapeños
1 (9-inch) refrigerated unbaked pie crust
½ cup (2 ounces) shredded Cheddar cheese

PREHEAT oven to 350°F. Melt butter in large saucepan over medium heat. Add onions, salt and thyme; stir to coat well. Cover; cook 5 minutes, stirring periodically to prevent onions from burning. Reduce heat; continue to cook and stir 15 minutes or until onions are golden brown and caramelized. Stir in salsa and jalapeños.

PLACE pie crust in 9-inch tart pan with removable bottom. Pierce dough several times with fork. Spread onion mixture evenly over crust.

BAKE 20 minutes or until crust begins to brown on sides. Sprinkle cheese evenly over tart. Bake 5 minutes longer. Remove from oven; let stand 5 minutes. Carefully remove from tart pan. Serve warm or at room temperature.

Prep Time: 20 minutes | Start to Finish: 1 hour

Tip: For a great brunch or lunch item, use ORTEGA® Salsa Verde in the tart filling and serve it with a salad of mixed greens.

Caramelized Onion Tart

Tofu Rigatoni Casserole
Makes 6 servings

3 cups uncooked rigatoni
4 cups loosely packed baby spinach
1 cup soft tofu
1 egg
¼ teaspoon salt
¼ teaspoon black pepper
¼ teaspoon ground nutmeg (optional)
1 can (about 14 ounces) diced tomatoes with basil, garlic and oregano
1 can (about 14 ounces) quartered artichokes, drained and chopped
2 cups (8 ounces) shredded Italian cheese blend, divided

1. Preheat oven to 350°F. Spray 11×7-inch baking dish with nonstick cooking spray.

2. Cook pasta in large saucepan according to package directions. Stir in spinach in bunches during last 2 minutes of cooking just until wilted. Drain; return to saucepan.

3. Meanwhile, combine tofu, egg, salt, pepper and nutmeg, if desired, in medium bowl; mix until blended. Fold tofu mixture into rigatoni. Add tomatoes, artichokes and 1½ cups cheese; mix well. Spoon into prepared baking dish.

4. Bake 20 minutes. Top with remaining ½ cup cheese. Bake 10 minutes or until cheese is browned.

Tofu Rigatoni Casserole

7-Layer Meatless Tortilla Pie

Makes 6 servings

2 cans (about 15 ounces each) pinto beans, rinsed and drained
1 cup PACE® Picante Sauce
¼ teaspoon garlic powder or 1 clove garlic, minced
2 tablespoons chopped fresh cilantro leaves
1 can (about 15 ounces) black beans, rinsed and drained
1 small tomato, chopped (about ½ cup)
7 flour tortillas (8-inch)
8 ounces shredded Cheddar cheese (about 2 cups)

1. Mash the pinto beans in a medium bowl with a fork. Stir in ¾ **cup** picante sauce and the garlic powder.

2. Stir the remaining picante sauce, cilantro, black beans and tomato in a medium bowl.

3. Place **1** tortilla onto a baking sheet. Spread ¾ **cup** pinto bean mixture over the tortilla to within ½-inch of the edge. Top with ¼ **cup** cheese. Top with **1** tortilla and ⅔ **cup** black bean mixture. Top with ¼ **cup** cheese. Repeat the layers twice more. Top with the remaining tortilla and spread with the remaining pinto bean mixture. Cover with aluminum foil.

4. Bake at 400°F. for 40 minutes or until the filling is hot. Uncover the pie. Top with the remaining cheese. Cut the pie into 6 wedges. Serve with additional picante sauce and sprinkle with additional cilantro, if desired.

Prep Time: 20 minutes | **Cook Time:** 40 minutes | **Total Time:** 1 hour

7-Layer Meatless Tortilla Pie

Baked Fusilli with Roasted Vegetables

Makes 6 to 8 servings

1 large eggplant, cut in half
3 medium red bell peppers, cut in half
1 large sweet onion, cut into quarters
2 tablespoons olive oil
1 container (15 ounces) ricotta cheese
   Salt and black pepper
1 package (about 16 ounces) fusilli pasta, cooked and drained
3 cups (12 ounces) shredded mozzarella cheese
½ cup grated Parmesan cheese

1. Preheat oven to 375°F. Line two baking sheets with foil. Place eggplant, peppers and onion, cut side down, on prepared baking sheets. Brush with olive oil; roast 30 minutes or until tender. Let cool; cut vegetables into bite-size pieces.

2. Combine ricotta and vegetables in large bowl; season with salt and black pepper. Add pasta; stir just until combined.

3. Spoon half of pasta mixture into 13×9-inch baking dish. Sprinkle with half of mozzarella and Parmesan. Repeat layers. Bake 25 minutes or until bubbly and browned.

Baked Fusilli with Roasted Vegetables

Cheese Soufflé
Makes 4 servings

¼ cup (½ stick) butter
¼ cup sweet rice flour
1½ cups milk, warmed to room temperature
¼ teaspoon salt
¼ teaspoon ground red pepper
⅛ teaspoon black pepper
6 eggs, separated
1 cup (4 ounces) shredded Cheddar cheese
Pinch cream of tartar (optional)

1. Preheat oven to 375°F. Grease 2-quart soufflé dish or 4 individual soufflé dishes.

2. Melt butter in large saucepan over medium-low heat. Add rice flour; whisk 2 minutes or until mixture just begins to color. Add milk, salt, red pepper and black pepper; whisk until mixture comes to a boil and thickens. Remove from heat. Stir in egg yolks, one at a time. Stir in cheese.

3. Place egg whites in clean large bowl with cream of tartar, if desired. Beat with electric mixer at high speed until egg whites form stiff peaks.

4. Fold egg whites into cheese mixture gently until almost combined. (Some streaks of white should remain.) Transfer mixture to prepared dish.

5. Bake 30 to 40 minutes or until puffed and browned. Skewer inserted in center should come out moist, but clean. Serve immediately.

Cheese Soufflé

Brunch Creations

Fiesta Breakfast Casserole
6 servings

- ½ pound bulk pork sausage
- 12 slices PEPPERIDGE FARM® White Sandwich Bread, cut into cubes (about 6 cups)
- 1½ cups shredded Cheddar cheese (about 6 ounces)
- 1 cup PACE® Picante Sauce
- 4 eggs
- ¾ cup milk

1. Cook the sausage in a 10-inch skillet over medium-high heat until well browned, stirring often to separate meat. Pour off any fat.

2. Spoon the sausage into a 2-quart shallow baking dish. Top with the bread cubes and cheese. Beat the picante sauce, eggs and milk in a medium bowl with a fork or whisk. Pour the picante sauce mixture over the bread mixture. Stir and press the bread mixture into the picante sauce mixture to coat. Cover and refrigerate for 2 hours or overnight.

3. Heat the oven to 350°F. Uncover the baking dish.

4. Bake for 45 minutes or until a knife inserted in the center comes out clean.

Tip: Prepare this dish the night before and pop it into the oven in the morning. It's great for when you have overnight guests. Add a simple side of sliced melon and breakfast is ready!

Prep Time: 15 minutes | Cook Time: 2 hours 45 minutes
Total Time: 3 hours

Mushroom and Arugula Quiche

Makes 4 to 6 servings

1 tablespoon olive oil
½ cup chopped onion
2 cloves garlic, minced
1½ cups sliced mushrooms (5 to 6 ounces)
1 package (5 ounces) DOLE® Baby Arugula with Baby Spinach Blend
1 cup (4 ounces) shredded Swiss cheese
¼ cup grated Parmesan cheese, divided
1 (9-inch) frozen deep-dish pie shell, thawed
4 eggs, well beaten
½ cup half-and-half
¼ teaspoon salt
   Pinch ground black pepper
   Pinch ground nutmeg

• Preheat oven to 375°F.

• Heat oil in large nonstick skillet over medium-high heat. Add onion and garlic; cook, stirring often, until tender, 3 to 4 minutes. Add mushrooms; cook, stirring occasionally, until excess moisture has evaporated and starts to brown, 4 to 5 minutes. Add the salad blend and cook, stirring until wilted and almost dry, 3 to 4 minutes. Remove from heat; cool slightly.

• Mix together cooled vegetables and Swiss cheese. Sprinkle ½ Parmesan cheese on bottom of pie shell. Top with vegetable mixture.

• Stir together eggs, half and half, salt and spices; pour into the pie shell. Sprinkle with remaining Parmesan cheese. Bake 30 minutes or until knife inserted near center comes out clean.

Prep Time: 15 minutes | Bake Time: 30 minutes

Mushroom and Arugula Quiche

Macaroni & Cheese with Bacon & Tomatoes

Makes 6 servings

     4 thick slices applewood-smoked bacon, diced
     2 tablespoons all-purpose flour
  2¼ cups milk
     ½ teaspoon salt
     ⅛ teaspoon cayenne pepper
  1¾ cups (7 ounces) SARGENTO® Shredded Colby-Jack Cheese, divided
     8 ounces (2 cups dry) multi-grain or regular elbow macaroni, cooked
        and drained
     1 can (14 ounces) fire-roasted diced tomatoes, drained

COOK bacon in a large saucepan over medium heat 5 to 6 minutes or until crisp, stirring frequently. Use a slotted spoon to transfer bacon to a paper towel; set aside.

ADD flour to drippings in pan; cook and stir 30 seconds. Add milk, salt and cayenne pepper; bring to a boil. Simmer 1 minute or until sauce thickens, stirring frequently. Remove from heat; stir in 1¼ cups cheese until melted. Stir in cooked macaroni and tomatoes. Transfer to a sprayed 9-inch baking dish or shallow 1½-quart casserole.

BAKE in a preheated 375°F oven 20 minutes or until heated through. Sprinkle reserved bacon and remaining cheese over macaroni; continue to bake 5 minutes or until cheese is melted.

Prep Time: **15 minutes** | Cook Time: **25 minutes**

Macaroni & Cheese with Bacon & Tomatoes

Ham 'n' Apple Breakfast Casserole

Makes 6 servings

1 package (15 ounces) refrigerated pie crusts (2 crusts)
1 pound thinly sliced ham, cut into bite-size pieces
1 can (about 21 ounces) apple pie filling
1 cup (4 ounces) shredded sharp Cheddar cheese
¼ cup plus 1 teaspoon sugar, divided
½ teaspoon ground cinnamon

1. Preheat oven to 425°F.

2. Place one crust in 9-inch pie pan, allowing edges to hang over sides. Arrange half of ham pieces in bottom; spoon apple pie filling over ham. Arrange remaining ham on top of apples; sprinkle with cheese.

3. Mix ¼ cup sugar and cinnamon in small bowl; sprinkle evenly over cheese. Arrange second crust over filling and crimp edges together. Brush crust lightly with water and sprinkle with remaining 1 teaspoon sugar. Cut slits for steam to escape.

4. Bake 20 to 25 minutes or until crust is golden brown. Cool 15 minutes before serving.

 Tip: This breakfast casserole can be assembled the night before, covered and refrigerated, then baked the next morning.

Ham 'n' Apple Breakfast Casserole

Egg and Green Chile Rice Casserole

Makes 4 servings

¾ cup uncooked instant brown rice
½ cup chopped green onions
½ teaspoon ground cumin
1 can (4 ounces) chopped mild green chiles, drained
⅛ teaspoon salt
4 eggs, beaten
½ cup (2 ounces) shredded sharp Cheddar cheese or
   Mexican cheese blend
¼ cup pico de gallo
1 medium lime, quartered

1. Preheat oven to 350°F. Lightly coat 8-inch square baking dish with nonstick cooking spray.

2. Cook rice according to package directions. Remove from heat; stir in green onions and cumin. Transfer to prepared baking dish.

3. Sprinkle chiles and salt evenly over rice mixture. Pour eggs evenly over top. Bake 30 to 35 minutes or until center is set.

4. Sprinkle with cheese. Bake 3 minutes or until cheese is melted. Let stand 5 minutes before cutting into squares. Serve with pico de gallo and lime wedges.

Egg and Green Chile Rice Casserole

Blueberry-Orange French Toast Casserole

Makes 4 servings

½ cup sugar
½ cup milk
2 eggs
4 egg whites
1 tablespoon grated orange peel
½ teaspoon vanilla
6 slices whole wheat bread, cut into 1-inch pieces
1 cup fresh blueberries

1. Preheat oven to 350°F. Coat 8-inch square baking dish with nonstick cooking spray.

2. Whisk sugar and milk in medium bowl until dissolved. Whisk in eggs, egg whites, orange peel and vanilla. Add bread and blueberries; toss to coat. Let stand 5 minutes.

3. Bake 40 to 45 minutes or until bread is browned and center is almost set. Let stand 5 minutes before serving.

Blueberry-Orange French Toast Casserole

Bacon and Eggs Brunch Casserole

Makes 6 servings

1 tube (8 ounces) refrigerated crescent roll dough
6 eggs
½ cup milk
1 cup (4 ounces) SARGENTO® Chef Style Shredded Mild
    Cheddar Cheese
8 slices bacon, diced and cooked crisp

SPRAY a 13×9-inch baking pan with non-stick cooking spray. Unroll dough and press into bottom of pan. Bake in preheated 350°F oven 10 minutes.

BEAT together eggs and milk in medium bowl. Pour over partially baked dough. Sprinkle with cheese and bacon; return to oven and bake 25 minutes more or until center is set.

Prep Time: 15 minutes | Cook Time: 35 minutes

Bacon and Eggs Brunch Casserole

Chile-Corn Quiche

Makes 6 servings

1 unbaked 9-inch pie crust
1 can (8¾ ounces) whole kernel corn, drained, *or* 1 cup frozen whole kernel corn, thawed
1 can (4 ounces) diced mild green chiles, drained
¼ cup thinly sliced green onions
1 cup (4 ounces) shredded Monterey Jack cheese
1½ cups half-and-half
3 eggs
½ teaspoon salt
½ teaspoon ground cumin

1. Preheat oven to 450°F. Line crust with foil; fill with dried beans or rice. Bake 10 minutes. Remove foil and beans. Bake 5 minutes or until lightly browned. Cool. *Reduce oven temperature to 375°F.*

2. Combine corn, chiles and green onions in small bowl. Spoon into crust; top with cheese. Whisk half-and-half, eggs, salt and cumin in medium bowl; pour over cheese.

3. Bake 35 to 45 minutes or until filling is puffed and knife inserted into center comes out clean. Let stand 10 minutes before serving.

Chile-Corn Quiche

Breakfast Casserole
Makes 6 to 8 servings

6 large eggs, beaten
½ cup sour cream
1 can (15 ounces) VEG•ALL® Original Mixed Vegetables, drained
1 cup frozen cubed hash brown potatoes, thawed
1 cup smoked sausage links, chopped
1 cup shredded pepper-jack cheese
2 tablespoons canned jalapeño pepper slices
1 cup broken tortilla chips

Preheat oven to 350°F.

In medium bowl, combine eggs and sour cream until smooth. Fold in remaining ingredients except tortilla chips.

Transfer mixture to greased 11×7-inch baking dish. Bake for 25 to 30 minutes or until eggs are set and puffed.

Top with tortilla chips and bake an additional 5 minutes. Serve with additional sour cream on the side, if desired.

Serve with fresh fruit for breakfast or brunch.

Variation: For a milder flavor, substitute chopped fresh cilantro for the sliced jalapeño peppers.

Breakfast Casserole

Biscuit and Sausage Bake

Makes 6 servings

   2 cups biscuit baking mix
½ cup milk
   1 egg
   1 teaspoon vanilla
   1 cup fresh or frozen blueberries
   6 fully cooked breakfast sausage links, thawed if frozen
      Warm maple syrup

1. Preheat oven to 350°F. Coat 8-inch square baking pan with nonstick cooking spray.

2. Whisk baking mix, milk, egg and vanilla in medium bowl. Gently fold in blueberries. (Batter will be stiff.) Spread batter in prepared pan.

3. Cut each sausage link into small pieces; sprinkle over batter.

4. Bake 22 minutes or until top is lightly browned. Cut into squares; serve with maple syrup.

Prep Time: 10 minutes | Bake Time: 22 minutes

Biscuit and Sausage Bake

Parmesan Pasta Frittata

Makes 6 servings

3 eggs
1 cup whipping cream
1¼ cups (5 ounces) SARGENTO® ARTISAN BLENDS™ Shredded
   Parmesan Cheese, divided
3 cups cooked, rinsed and drained spaghetti pasta
   (7 ounces uncooked)
2 cups diced grilled or roasted mixed vegetables, such as bell peppers,
   asparagus and zucchini squash
1 teaspoon salt
¼ teaspoon black pepper
1 tablespoon olive oil

LIGHTLY BEAT eggs in a large bowl. Add cream and 1 cup of the cheese; mix well. Stir in pasta, vegetables, salt and pepper; mix well.

HEAT oil in an ovenproof (wrap handle in foil) 12-inch nonstick skillet over medium-high heat until hot. Add pasta mixture; pat down into a firm layer. Cook 3 to 4 minutes or until bottom of frittata is golden brown.

TRANSFER skillet to a preheated 400°F oven. Bake 15 to 17 minutes or until center is set. Remove from oven; slide a spatula around edges to loosen frittata. Place a large serving plate or cutting board over skillet; invert frittata onto serving plate; top with remaining ¼ cup cheese. Let stand 5 minutes; cut into wedges.

Prep Time: 20 minutes | Cook Time: 21 minutes

Parmesan Pasta Frittata

Hash Brown Breakfast Casserole

Makes 6 servings

3 cups refrigerated or frozen shredded hash brown potatoes, thawed
1½ cups (6 ounces) finely chopped ham
¾ cup (3 ounces) shredded Cheddar cheese
¼ cup sliced green onions
1 can (12 ounces) evaporated milk
1 tablespoon all-purpose flour
4 eggs, beaten
½ teaspoon black pepper

1. Lightly spray 8-inch square baking dish with nonstick cooking spray.

2. Layer potatoes, ham, cheese and green onions in prepared dish.

3. Gradually whisk evaporated milk into flour in medium bowl. Stir in eggs and pepper. Pour into prepared baking dish. Cover and refrigerate 4 to 24 hours.

4. Preheat oven to 350°F. Bake, uncovered, 55 to 60 minutes or until knife inserted into center comes out clean.

5. Remove from oven; let stand 10 minutes before serving.

Prep Time: **10 minutes** | Chill Time: **4 hours** | Bake Time: **55 minutes**

Desserts

Table of Contents

Pie Perfection

Maple Walnut Pie
Makes 8 servings

- **1 cup maple syrup**
- **3 eggs**
- **½ cup packed dark brown sugar**
- **1 tablespoon butter, melted**
- **1 teaspoon vanilla**
- **¼ teaspoon salt**
- **1 cup coarsely chopped walnuts**
- **1 (9-inch) unbaked deep-dish pie shell**
- **Whipped topping or whipped cream (optional)**

1. Preheat oven to 350°F.

2. Beat syrup, eggs, brown sugar, butter, vanilla and salt in large bowl with electric mixer at medium speed until well blended. Stir in walnuts. Pour filling into unbaked pie shell.

3. Bake 40 to 45 minutes or until center is firm. Cool 2 hours on wire rack. Top with dollops of whipped topping, if desired. Store in refrigerator.

Strawberry Rhubarb Pie
Makes 8 servings

     Pie dough for a 2-crust pie (recipe follows)
    4 cups sliced (1-inch pieces) fresh rhubarb
    3 cups sliced fresh strawberries
   1½ cups sugar
     ½ cup cornstarch
    2 tablespoons quick-cooking tapioca
    1 tablespoon grated lemon peel
   ¼ teaspoon ground allspice
    1 egg, lightly beaten

1. Preheat oven to 425°F. Roll out half of pie dough; place in 9-inch pie plate. Trim dough; flute edges, sealing to edge of pie plate. Set aside.

2. Place rhubarb and strawberries in large bowl. Combine sugar, cornstarch, tapioca, lemon peel and allspice in medium bowl; mix well. Sprinkle sugar mixture over fruit; toss to coat well. Fill pie shell with fruit. (Do not mound in center.)

3. Roll out remaining pastry to 10-inch square. Cut into ½-inch-wide strips. Arrange in lattice design over fruit. Brush pastry with egg.

4. Bake 50 minutes or until filling is thick and bubbly. Cool on wire rack. Serve warm or at room temperature.

Pie Dough for a 2-Crust Pie

  2½ cups all-purpose flour
    1 teaspoon salt
    1 teaspoon sugar
    1 cup (2 sticks) cold unsalted butter, cubed
   ⅓ cup cold water

1. Combine flour, salt and sugar in large bowl. Cut in butter using pastry blender or two knives until mixture resembles coarse crumbs.

2. Add 2 tablespoons water; stir to blend. Repeat with remaining water. Knead dough just until it comes together. Divide dough in half. Shape each half into disc; wrap in plastic wrap. Refrigerate at least 1 hour or up to 2 days.

Strawberry Rhubarb Pie

Chocolate Walnut Toffee Tart

Makes 12 servings

2 cups all-purpose flour
1¼ cups plus 3 tablespoons sugar, divided
¾ cup (1½ sticks) butter, cut into pieces
2 egg yolks
1¼ cups whipping cream
1 teaspoon ground cinnamon
2 teaspoons vanilla
2 cups coarsely chopped walnuts
1¼ cups semisweet chocolate chips or chunks, divided

1. Place piece of foil in bottom of oven to catch any spills. Preheat oven to 325°F.

2. Place flour and 3 tablespoons sugar in food processor; pulse just until mixed. Scatter butter over flour mixture; process 20 seconds. Add egg yolks; process 10 seconds (mixture may be crumbly).

3. Press dough firmly and evenly into ungreased 10-inch tart pan with removable bottom or 10-inch pie pan. Bake 10 minutes or until surface is no longer shiny. Remove from oven.

4. *Increase oven temperature to 375°F.* Combine remaining 1¼ cups sugar, cream and cinnamon in large saucepan; bring to a boil. Reduce heat to medium-low; simmer 10 minutes, stirring frequently. Remove from heat; stir in vanilla.

5. Sprinkle walnuts and 1 cup chocolate chips evenly over crust. Pour cream mixture over top. Bake 35 to 40 minutes or until filling is bubbly and crust is lightly browned. Cool completely in pan on wire rack.

6. Place remaining ¼ cup chocolate chips in small resealable food storage bag. Microwave on HIGH 20 seconds; knead bag until chocolate is melted. Cut small hole in one corner of bag; drizzle chocolate over tart.

Note: Tart may be made up to 5 days in advance. Cover with plastic wrap and store at room temperature.

Prep Time: 25 minutes | Bake Time: 40 minutes

Chocolate Walnut Toffee Tart

Dreamy Orange Pie
Makes 10 servings

8 whole honey graham crackers, crushed (1½ cups)
2 tablespoons butter, melted
1 pint vanilla ice cream, softened
1 pint orange sherbet, softened
10 tablespoons thawed frozen whipped topping
10 mandarin orange slices

1. Preheat oven to 350°F. Spray 9-inch springform baking pan with nonstick cooking spray.

2. Combine crumbs and butter in medium bowl. Gently press crumb mixture on bottom and ½ inch up side of pan. Bake 8 to 10 minutes or until lightly browned. Cool completely on wire rack.

3. Spread ice cream evenly in cooled crust. Freeze 30 minutes or until firm to the touch. Spread orange sherbet evenly over ice cream; freeze at least 1 hour or until ready to serve.

4. To serve, run knife carefully around edge of pan; remove side of pan. Cut into 10 slices. Top each slice with 1 tablespoon whipped topping and 1 orange slice.

Dreamy Orange Pie

Deep-Dish Blueberry Pie

Makes 9 servings

Pie Dough for a 2-Crust Pie (page 196)
6 cups fresh blueberries *or* **2 (16 ounce) packages frozen blueberries,**
thawed and drained
2 tablespoons lemon juice
1¼ cups sugar
3 tablespoons quick-cooking tapioca
¼ teaspoon ground cinnamon
1 tablespoon butter, cut into tiny pieces

1. Prepare Pie Dough for a 2-Crust Pie. Preheat oven to 400°F.

2. Place blueberries in large bowl and sprinkle with lemon juice. Combine sugar, tapioca and cinnamon in small bowl; gently stir into blueberries until blended.

3. Roll 1 disc dough into 12-inch circle on lightly floured work surface. Fit dough into 9-inch deep-dish pie pan. Trim all but ½ inch of overhang. Pour blueberry mixture into pan; dot with butter.

4. Roll remaining disc dough into 10-inch circle. Using small cookie cutter or knife, cut 4 or 5 shapes from dough for vents. Lift and center dough over blueberry mixture in pie pan. Trim dough, leaving 1-inch border. Fold excess dough under and even with pan edge. Crimp edges with fork.

5. Bake 15 minutes. *Reduce oven temperature to 350°F.* Bake 40 minutes or until crust is golden brown. Cool on wire rack 30 minutes before serving.

Deep-Dish Blueberry Pie

Chocolate Cookie Pie

Makes 8 servings

20 chocolate sandwich cookies
1 cup whipping cream
1 (6-ounce) chocolate crumb pie crust

1. Place 14 cookies in resealable food storage bag and crush into coarse crumbs with rolling pin or mallet. Whip cream in large bowl with electric mixer at high speed until soft peaks form.

2. Stir cookie crumbs gently into whipped cream; spoon into crust. Garnish with remaining cookies. Cover and freeze until ready to serve. Let stand at room temperature 10 minutes before serving.

Sweet Potato Pie

Makes one 9-inch pie

1 pound sweet potatoes,* boiled and peeled
¼ cup (½ stick) butter or margarine
1 (14-ounce) can EAGLE BRAND® Sweetened Condensed Milk (NOT evaporated milk)
2 eggs
1 teaspoon grated orange rind
1 teaspoon vanilla extract
1 teaspoon ground cinnamon
1 teaspoon ground nutmeg
¼ teaspoon salt
1 (9-inch) unbaked pie crust

*For best results, use fresh sweet potatoes.

1. Preheat oven to 350°F. In large bowl, beat sweet potatoes and butter until smooth. Add EAGLE BRAND®, eggs, orange rind, vanilla, cinnamon, nutmeg and salt; mix well. Pour into crust.

2. Bake 40 minutes or until golden brown. Cool. Garnish as desired. Store leftovers covered in refrigerator.

Prep Time: 20 minutes | **Bake Time:** 40 minutes

Chocolate Cookie Pie

Banana Cream–Caramel Pie

Makes 8 servings

WHAT YOU NEED

2 bananas, sliced
1 OREO® Pie Crust (6-ounce)
⅓ cup PLANTERS® Walnut Pieces
3 tablespoons caramel ice cream topping
1 cup cold milk
1 package (3.4-ounce) JELL-O® Vanilla Flavor Instant Pudding
1 tub (8-ounce) COOL WHIP® Whipped Topping, thawed, divided
4 squares BAKER'S® Semi-Sweet Chocolate

MAKE IT

1. SPREAD bananas onto bottom of crust; top with nuts and ice cream topping.

2. BEAT milk and pudding mix in large bowl with whisk 2 minutes. Stir in half the COOL WHIP®; spoon into crust.

3 MICROWAVE chocolate in medium microwaveable bowl on HIGH 1½ minutes or until melted, stirring every 45 seconds. Add remaining COOL WHIP®; whisk until blended. Cool slightly; spread over pudding mixture. Refrigerate 4 hours.

Substitute: Prepare using JELL-O® Banana Instant Pudding.

Prep Time: 15 minutes (plus refrigerating)

Banana Cream-Caramel Pie

Buttermilk Pie

Makes 8 servings

1½ cups sugar
1 tablespoon cornstarch
3 eggs
½ cup buttermilk
¼ cup (½ stick) butter, melted
1 tablespoon lemon juice
1 teaspoon vanilla
1 (9-inch) graham cracker crust
Whipped cream (optional)

1. Preheat oven to 350°F.

2. Combine sugar and cornstarch in medium bowl. Whisk in eggs, buttermilk, butter, lemon juice and vanilla. Beat with electric mixer at medium speed until smooth. Pour into pie crust.

3. Bake 40 to 50 minutes or until set. Cool on wire rack. Refrigerate until ready to serve. Serve chilled with whipped cream, if desired.

Buttermilk Pie

Fresh Apple and Toffee Tart
Makes 2 tarts (8 servings each)

4 to 6 large tart apples such as Granny Smith
¼ cup granulated sugar
2 tablespoons cornstarch or all-purpose flour
½ teaspoon ground cinnamon
1 package (15-ounce box) refrigerated pie crusts, softened as
   directed on box
1⅓ cups (8-ounce package) HEATH BITS 'O BRICKLE® Toffee Bits,
   divided
2 teaspoons white decorator sugar crystals or granulated sugar,
   divided
Sweetened whipped cream or ice cream (optional)

1. Heat oven to 400°F. Peel and slice apples into thin slices. Toss apples with granulated sugar, cornstarch and cinnamon.

2. Unroll crusts; place each on ungreased cookie sheet. Sprinkle ⅓ cup toffee bits over each crust; press lightly into crust.

3. Starting 2 inches from the edge of the crust, arrange apple slices by overlapping slightly in a circular spiral toward the center of the crust. Sprinkle ⅓ cup of remaining toffee bits over tops. Fold 2-inch edge of crust over apples. Sprinkle each crust edge with 1 teaspoon sugar crystals.

4. Bake 25 to 30 minutes or until crust is golden. Cool slightly. Serve warm or cool with sweetened whipped cream or ice cream, if desired.

Note: Recipe may be halved.

Fresh Apple and Toffee Tart

Peanut Butter Cup Pie
Makes 10 servings

WHAT YOU NEED
1 package (8 ounces) PHILADELPHIA® Cream Cheese, softened
½ cup plus 1 tablespoon creamy peanut butter, divided
1 cup cold milk
1 package (3.4 ounces) JELL-O® Vanilla Flavor Instant Pudding
2½ cups thawed COOL WHIP® Whipped Topping, divided
1 OREO® Pie Crust (6 ounces)
3 squares BAKER'S® Semi-Sweet Chocolate

MAKE IT
1. BEAT cream cheese and ½ cup peanut butter until well blended. Add milk and dry pudding mix; beat 2 minutes. Whisk in 1 cup COOL WHIP®; spoon into crust. Refrigerate until ready to use.

2. MEANWHILE, microwave remaining COOL WHIP® and chocolate in microwaveable bowl on HIGH 1½ to 2 minutes or until chocolate is completely melted and mixture is well blended, stirring after each minute. Cool completely.

3. SPREAD chocolate mixture over pudding layer in crust. Microwave remaining peanut butter in small microwaveable bowl 30 seconds; stir. Drizzle over pie. Refrigerate 4 hours or until firm.

Substitute: Prepare using JELL-O® Chocolate Instant Pudding.

Prep Time: 15 minutes plus refrigerating

Peanut Butter Cup Pie

Easy Cherry Cream Pie

Makes 8 servings

1 pint vanilla ice cream, softened
½ (16-ounce) package frozen dark sweet cherries, chopped
1 cup whipping cream
1 tablespoon powdered sugar
⅛ teaspoon almond extract
1 (6-ounce) chocolate crumb or graham cracker pie crust

1. Combine ice cream and cherries in large bowl just until blended.

2. Beat cream, powdered sugar and almond extract in medium bowl with electric mixer at medium speed until soft peaks form.

3. Spoon ice cream mixture into pie crust. Spoon whipped cream mixture evenly on top. Freeze 1 hour or until firm. Let stand at room temperature 10 minutes before serving.

Prep Time: 10 minutes

Brownie Bottom Ice Cream Pie

Makes 8 servings

1 package (about 16 ounces) refrigerated brownie batter
5 to 6 cups favorite flavor ice cream, softened
1 jar (8 ounces) hot fudge topping

1. Preheat oven to 350°F. Spray 9-inch pie pan with nonstick cooking spray. Let batter stand at room temperature 5 minutes to soften.

2. Place batter in prepared pan; use dampened hands to spread batter over bottom and halfway up side of pan. Bake about 20 minutes or until toothpick inserted into center comes out clean. Cool completely in pan on wire rack.

3. Top brownie layer with ice cream, spreading to edge of pie pan. Serve immediately or cover with plastic wrap and freeze up to several hours. (If frozen, let pie stand at room temperature 10 minutes to soften.) Drizzle with hot fudge topping before serving.

Easy Cherry Cream Pie

Chocolate Chip Cookie Dough Cheesepie

Makes 8 servings

Cookie Dough (recipe follows)
2 packages (3 ounces *each*) cream cheese, softened
⅓ cup sugar
⅓ cup dairy sour cream
1 egg
½ teaspoon vanilla extract
1 packaged chocolate crumb crust (6 ounces)

1. Prepare Cookie Dough.

2. Heat oven to 350°F.

3. Beat cream cheese and sugar in small bowl on medium speed of mixer until smooth; blend in sour cream, egg and vanilla. Pour into crust. Drop cookie dough by teaspoons evenly onto cream cheese mixture.

4. Bake 35 to 40 minutes or until almost set in center. Cool completely on wire rack. Cover; refrigerate leftover pie.

Cookie Dough

2 tablespoons butter or margarine, softened
¼ cup packed light brown sugar
¼ cup all-purpose flour
1 tablespoon water
¼ teaspoon vanilla extract
1 cup HERSHEY₀S SPECIAL DARK® Chocolate Chips or
    HERSHEY₀S Semi-Sweet Chocolate Chips

Beat butter and brown sugar in small bowl until fluffy. Add flour, water and vanilla; beat until blended. Stir in chocolate chips.

Chocolate Chip Cookie Dough Cheesepie

Butterscotch Pecan Pie

Makes 10 servings

1 *unbaked* **9-inch (4-cup volume) deep-dish pie shell***
1⅔ cups (11-ounce package) NESTLÉ® TOLL HOUSE® Butterscotch
   Flavored Morsels, *divided*
¾ cup light corn syrup
3 eggs, room temperature
1 tablespoon all-purpose flour
¼ teaspoon salt
1½ cups pecan halves, coarsely chopped
1½ cups whipped cream (optional)

If using frozen pie shell, use deep-dish style. Do not thaw. Bake on baking sheet.

PREHEAT oven to 350°F.

MELT *1⅓ cups* morsels in medium, uncovered microwave-safe bowl on MEDIUM-HIGH (70%) power for 1 minute; STIR. Morsels may retain some of their shape. If necessary, microwave at additional 10- to 15-second intervals, stirring just until morsels are melted.

BEAT melted morsels, corn syrup, eggs, flour and salt on medium speed with electric mixer until smooth. Stir in pecans. Pour pecan mixture into pie shell.

BAKE for 40 to 45 minutes or until knife inserted into center comes out with little bits of filling attached. If browning too quickly, cover with foil. Cool on wire rack for 2 hours. Refrigerate 1 hour or until serving time.

TO GARNISH AND SERVE
LINE baking sheet with wax paper.

PLACE *remaining* morsels in *heavy-duty* plastic bag. Microwave on MEDIUM-HIGH (70%) power for 30 to 45 seconds; knead. Microwave at 10- to 15-second intervals, kneading until smooth. Cut tiny corner from bag. Drizzle 10 designs about 2 inches high and wide onto prepared baking sheet. Refrigerate for 5 to 10 minutes or until firm.

PLACE 10 dollops of whipped cream around edge of pie. Remove drizzle designs from refrigerator. With tip of knife, gently remove designs from wax paper and insert, standing up, into dollops. Serve immediately.

Tip: ⅓ cup NESTLÉ® TOLL HOUSE® Semi-Sweet Chocolate Morsels can also be melted and made into drizzle designs instead of the Butterscotch Flavored Morsels.

Butterscotch Pecan Pie

Classic Cakes

Nutty Toffee Coffee Cake

Makes 12 to 16 servings

1⅓ cups (8-ounce package) HEATH® BITS 'O BRICKLE® Toffee Bits, divided

⅓ cup plus ¾ cup packed light brown sugar, divided

2¼ cups all-purpose flour, divided

9 tablespoons butter or margarine, softened and divided

¾ cup granulated sugar

2 teaspoons baking powder

½ teaspoon ground cinnamon

¼ teaspoon salt

1¼ cups milk

1 egg

1 teaspoon vanilla extract

¾ cup chopped nuts

1. Heat oven to 350°F. Grease and flour 13×9×2-inch baking pan. Stir together ½ cup toffee bits, ⅓ cup brown sugar, ¼ cup flour and 3 tablespoons butter. Stir until crumbly; set aside.

2. Combine remaining 2 cups flour, granulated sugar, remaining ¾ cup brown sugar, remaining 6 tablespoons butter, baking powder, cinnamon and salt in large mixer bowl; mix until well blended. Gradually add milk, egg and vanilla, beating until thoroughly blended. Stir in remaining toffee bits and nuts. Spread batter in prepared pan.

3. Sprinkle reserved crumb topping over batter. Bake 30 to 35 minutes or until wooden pick inserted in center comes out clean. Serve warm or cool.

Strawberry Chocolate Roll

Makes 8 to 12 servings

 3 eggs, separated
½ cup sugar
 5 ounces semisweet chocolate, melted
⅓ cup water
 1 teaspoon vanilla
¾ cup all-purpose flour
 1 teaspoon baking powder
½ teaspoon baking soda
¼ teaspoon salt
   Unsweetened cocoa powder
½ cup seedless strawberry jam
 2 pints strawberry ice cream, softened

1. Preheat oven to 350°F. Line 15×10-inch jelly roll pan with foil, extending foil 1 inch over ends of pan. Grease and flour foil.

2. Beat egg yolks and sugar in large bowl with electric mixer at medium speed until light and fluffy. Beat in melted chocolate. Add water and vanilla; mix until smooth. Sift flour, baking powder, baking soda and salt in small bowl; add to chocolate mixture.

3. Using clean beaters, beat egg whites in another large bowl at high speed until soft peaks form. Gently fold in chocolate mixture. Pour into prepared pan.

4. Bake 8 to 9 minutes or until toothpick inserted into center comes out clean. Carefully loosen sides of cake from foil. Invert cake onto towel sprinkled with cocoa. Peel off foil. Starting at short end, roll warm cake jelly-roll-style with towel inside. Cool completely on wire rack.

5. Unroll cake and remove towel. Spread cake with jam. Spread ice cream over jam, leaving a ¼-inch border. Roll up cake. Wrap tightly in plastic wrap or foil. Freeze 1 hour or until ready to serve. Allow cake to stand at room temperature 10 minutes before cutting and serving.

Strawberry Chocolate Roll

Coconut Cupcakes

Makes 36 cupcakes

1 package DUNCAN HINES® Moist Deluxe® Butter Recipe Golden Cake Mix
3 eggs
1 cup (8 ounces) dairy sour cream
⅔ cup cream of coconut
¼ cup (½ stick) butter or margarine, softened
2 containers (16 ounces each) DUNCAN HINES® Creamy Home-Style Coconut Supreme Frosting

1. Preheat oven to 375°F. Place paper liners into 36 standard (2½-inch) muffin cups.

2. Combine cake mix, eggs, sour cream, cream of coconut and butter in large bowl. Beat at low speed with electric mixer until blended. Beat at medium speed 4 minutes. Fill paper liners half full. Bake at 375°F for 17 to 19 minutes or until toothpick inserted into centers comes out clean. Cool in pans 5 minutes. Remove to cooling racks. Cool completely. Frost cupcakes. Garnish with toasted coconut, if desired.

Note: To toast coconut, spread evenly on baking sheet. Bake at 350°F for 3 minutes. Stir and bake 1 to 2 minutes longer or until golden brown.

Coconut Cupcakes

Banana-Nut Cake

Makes one 2-layer cake

2½ cups all-purpose flour
1 teaspoon salt
¾ teaspoon baking powder
¾ teaspoon baking soda
1⅔ cups sugar
⅔ cup shortening
2 eggs
2 to 3 mashed ripe bananas (about 1¼ cups)
1 teaspoon vanilla
⅔ cup buttermilk, divided
1 cup chopped walnuts
Browned Butter Frosting (page 228)

1. Preheat oven to 375°F. Grease and flour two (9-inch) round cake pans.

2. Combine flour, salt, baking powder and baking soda in medium bowl.

3. Beat sugar and shortening in large bowl with electric mixer at high speed until light and fluffy. Add eggs, one at a time, beating well after each addition. Blend in bananas and vanilla.

4. Add flour mixture alternately with buttermilk, beating well after each addition. Stir in walnuts. Pour evenly into prepared pans.

5. Bake 30 to 35 minutes or until toothpick inserted into centers comes out clean. Cool in pans on wire racks 10 minutes. Loosen edges; remove to racks to cool completely.

6. Fill and frost with Browned Butter Frosting. Run pastry comb across top and around side of cake, if desired, for ridged effect.

continued on page 228

Banana-Nut Cake

Banana-Nut Cake, continued

Browned Butter Frosting

¾ cup (1½ sticks) butter
5½ cups sifted powdered sugar
1½ teaspoons vanilla
    Dash salt
½ cup plus 1 tablespoon whipping cream or half-and-half

Melt butter in heavy 1-quart saucepan over medium heat; cook and stir until butter is light amber in color. Cool butter slightly. Beat browned butter, powdered sugar, vanilla, salt and ½ cup cream in large bowl with electric mixer at medium speed until smooth and of spreading consistency. Stir in remaining 1 tablespoon cream if frosting is too stiff.

Chocolate Tres Leches Cake
Makes 16 servings

WHAT YOU NEED
    1 package (2-layer size) white cake mix
    4 squares BAKER'S® Semi-Sweet Chocolate, divided
    1 can (14-ounce) sweetened condensed milk
    1 can (12-ounce) evaporated milk
    ½ cup BREAKSTONE'S® or KNUDSEN® Sour Cream
    1 cup thawed COOL WHIP® Whipped Topping

MAKE IT
1. PREPARE cake batter and bake in 13×9-inch pan as directed on package. Cool cake in pan 10 minutes. Pierce cake with large fork at ½-inch intervals.

2. MELT 3 chocolate squares; set aside. Blend milks and sour cream in blender until smooth. Add melted chocolate; blend well. Slowly pour over cake, re-piercing cake as needed until milk mixture is absorbed. Refrigerate 1 hour.

3. MAKE curls or shavings from remaining chocolate square. Frost top of cake with COOL WHIP®; top with chocolate curls. Refrigerate leftovers.

Chocolate Tres Leches Cake

Slow Cooker Sticky Caramel Pumpkin Cake

Makes 8 servings

      2 cups all-purpose flour
      2 teaspoons baking powder
      1 teaspoon baking soda
      ½ teaspoon salt
      ½ teaspoon pumpkin pie spice or ground cinnamon
    1⅓ cups sugar
      1 cup (2 sticks) unsalted butter, at room temperature
      4 eggs, at room temperature
      1 can (15 ounces) solid-pack pumpkin
      1 jar (16 ounces) caramel sauce or caramel ice cream topping
        Vanilla ice cream (optional)

SLOW COOKER DIRECTIONS

1. Coat 4½-quart slow cooker with nonstick cooking spray.

2. Whisk flour, baking powder, baking soda, salt and pumpkin pie spice in large bowl. Beat sugar and butter in another large bowl with electric mixer at high speed about 3 minutes or until light and fluffy. Add eggs, one at a time, beating well after each addition. Beat in pumpkin. Gradually add flour mixture and beat at low speed until smooth. Spread evenly in slow cooker.

3. Cover; cook on HIGH 2 to 2½ hours or until toothpick inserted into center of cake comes out clean. Drizzle ½ cup caramel sauce over cake.

4. Spoon into bowls and serve warm with ice cream, if desired. Drizzle with additional caramel sauce.

Serving Suggestion: For a fancier presentation, trim a sheet of parchment paper to fit the bottom of the stoneware insert. Spray the insert with nonstick cooking spray, then line with trimmed parchment paper and spray again. Proceed as above but before drizzling with caramel sauce, place a plate upside-down on top of the stoneware and invert cake onto plate. Remove parchment paper and invert onto serving plate.

Slow Cooker Sticky Caramel Pumpkin Cake

Chilled Raspberry Cheesecake
Makes 10 to 12 servings

1½ cups vanilla wafer crumbs (about 45 wafers, crushed)
⅓ cup HERSHEY₀S Cocoa
⅓ cup powdered sugar
⅓ cup butter or margarine, melted
1 package (10 ounces) frozen raspberries (about 2½ cups), thawed
1 envelope unflavored gelatin
½ cup cold water
½ cup boiling water
2 packages (8 ounces each) cream cheese, softened
½ cup granulated sugar
1 teaspoon vanilla extract
3 tablespoons seedless red raspberry preserves
Chocolate Whipped Cream (recipe follows)

1. Heat oven to 350°F.

2. Stir together vanilla wafer crumbs, ⅓ cup cocoa and ⅓ cup powdered sugar in medium bowl; stir in melted butter. Press mixture onto bottom and 1½ inches up side of 9-inch springform pan. Bake 10 minutes; cool completely.

3. Purée and strain raspberries; set aside. Sprinkle gelatin over cold water in small bowl; let stand several minutes to soften. Add boiling water; stir until gelatin dissolves completely and mixture is clear. Beat cream cheese, granulated sugar and 1 teaspoon vanilla in large bowl until smooth. Gradually add raspberry purée and gelatin, mixing thoroughly; pour into prepared crust.

4. Refrigerate several hours or overnight. Loosen cake from side of pan with knife; remove side of pan. Stir raspberry preserves to soften; spread over cheesecake top. Garnish with Chocolate Whipped Cream. Cover; refrigerate leftovers.

Chocolate Whipped Cream: Stir together ½ cup powdered sugar and ¼ cup HERSHEY₀S Cocoa in medium bowl. Add 1 cup (½ pint) cold whipping cream and 1 teaspoon vanilla extract; beat until stiff.

Chilled Raspberry Cheesecake

Chocolate Hazelnut Delight

Makes 12 servings

1 package (about 18 ounces) devil's food cake mix
1 cup finely chopped toasted hazelnuts
1 package (4-serving size) instant chocolate pudding and pie filling mix
1⅓ cups water
3 eggs
½ cup vegetable oil
2 teaspoons vanilla, divided
4 cups powdered sugar
1 cup (2 sticks) unsalted butter, softened
4 to 6 tablespoons milk
1½ cups chocolate hazelnut spread, divided
16 whole toasted hazelnuts (optional)

1. Preheat oven to 350°F. Spray three 9-inch cake pans with nonstick cooking spray.

2. Combine cake mix, chopped hazelnuts and pudding mix in large bowl; mix well. Add water, eggs, oil and vanilla; beat with electric mixer at medium speed 2 minutes or until smooth. Divide batter evenly among prepared pans. Bake 18 to 20 minutes or until toothpick inserted into centers comes out clean. Cool completely on wire rack.

3. Beat powdered sugar and butter in medium bowl at low speed until smooth. Add milk and remaining 1 teaspoon vanilla; beat until light and fluffy. Add 1 cup hazelnut spread; beat until smooth.

4. Microwave remaining ½ cup hazelnut spread in small microwavable bowl on HIGH 15 seconds or until warm but not melted. Spread evenly over tops of cake layers; cool slightly. Place one layer on serving plate and spread with frosting. Repeat with remaining layers. Frost cake with remaining frosting. Pipe 16 rosettes of frosting around cake and place 1 toasted hazelnut on each rosette, if desired.

Chocolate Hazelnut Delight

Milano® Cookie Caramel Ice Cream Cake

Makes 8 servings

1 package (6 ounces) PEPPERIDGE FARM® Milano® Cookies
3 cups vanilla or chocolate ice cream, softened
⅓ cup prepared caramel topping

1. Line an 8-inch round cake pan with plastic wrap.

2. Cut the cookies in half crosswise and arrange around the edge of the pan. Place the remaining cookies in the bottom of the pan.

3. Spread **1½ cups** ice cream over the cookies. Drizzle with the caramel topping. Spread the remaining ice cream over the caramel topping. Cover and freeze for 6 hours or until the ice cream is firm.

4. Uncover the pan and invert the cake onto a serving plate. Serve with additional caramel topping.

Variation: Substitute chocolate topping for the caramel topping.

Freeze Time: 6 hours | **Prep Time:** 20 minutes
Total Time: 6 hours 20 minutes

Milano® Cookie Caramel Ice Cream Cake

Carrot Cream Cheese Cupcakes

Makes 14 jumbo cupcakes

1 package (8 ounces) cream cheese, softened
¼ cup powdered sugar
1 package (about 18 ounces) spice cake mix, plus ingredients to
    prepare mix
2 cups grated carrots
2 tablespoons finely chopped candied ginger
1 container (16 ounces) cream cheese frosting
3 tablespoons maple syrup
    Orange peel strips (optional)

1. Preheat oven to 350°F. Spray 14 jumbo (3½-inch) muffin cups with nonstick cooking spray or line with paper baking cups.

2. Beat cream cheese and powdered sugar in large bowl with electric mixer at medium speed 1 minute or until light and fluffy. Cover and refrigerate.

3. Prepare cake mix according to package directions; stir in carrots and ginger. Spoon batter into prepared muffin cups, filling one third full (about ¼ cup batter). Place 1 tablespoon cream cheese mixture in center of each cup. Top evenly with remaining batter (muffin cups should be two thirds full).

4. Bake 25 to 28 minutes or until toothpick inserted into centers comes out clean. Cool cupcakes in pans 10 minutes. Remove to wire racks; cool completely.

5. Combine frosting and maple syrup in medium bowl until well blended. Frost cupcakes; garnish with orange peel.

Carrot Cream Cheese Cupcakes

No-Bake Chocolate Cake Roll

Makes about 12 servings

1 package (4-serving size) vanilla instant pudding and pie filling mix
3 tablespoons HERSHEY₅S Cocoa, divided
1 cup milk
1 tub (8 ounces) frozen non-dairy whipped topping, thawed and
   divided
1 package (9 ounces) crisp chocolate wafers
   HERSHEY₅S HUGS® BRAND Candies and HERSHEY₅S KISSES®
   BRAND Milk Chocolates

1. Combine pudding mix and 2 tablespoons cocoa in small bowl. Add milk; beat on low speed of mixer until smooth and thickened. Fold in 1 cup whipped topping, blending well.

2. Spread about 1 tablespoon pudding mixture onto top of each chocolate wafer; put wafers together in stacks of 4 or 5. On foil, stand wafers on edge to make one long roll. Wrap tightly; refrigerate 5 to 6 hours.

3. Sift remaining 1 tablespoon cocoa over remaining 2½ cups whipped topping; blend well. Unwrap roll; place on serving tray. Spread whipped topping mixture over entire roll. Remove wrappers from candies; place on roll to garnish. To serve, slice diagonally at 45-degree angle. Cover; refrigerate leftover dessert.

No-Bake Chocolate Cake Roll

Fresh & Fruity

Cherry Turnovers
Makes 12 turnovers

1 can (21 ounces) cherry pie filling
2 teaspoons grated orange peel
1 package (15 ounces) refrigerated pie crusts
1 egg yolk
1 tablespoon milk
1 tablespoon sugar
½ teaspoon ground cinnamon

1. Preheat oven to 375°F.

2. Combine pie filling and orange peel in medium bowl.

3. Roll 1 pie crust on floured surface to 12-inch circle. Cut out 6 circles with 4-inch cookie cutter. Repeat with second crust.

4. Combine egg yolk and milk in small bowl. Combine sugar and cinnamon in another small bowl.

5. Spoon scant tablespoon pie filling mixture onto center of each pastry circle. Brush edges of pastry circles with egg yolk mixture; fold pastry circles in half to enclose filling. Press edges together with fork to seal. Place on ungreased baking sheet. Cut thin vents into tops of turnovers. Brush tops with remaining egg yolk mixture; sprinkle with cinnamon-sugar.

6. Bake 18 to 20 minutes or until golden brown. Remove to wire rack; cool slightly. Serve warm.

Summertime Fruit Medley
Makes 8 servings

2 large ripe peaches, peeled and sliced
2 large ripe nectarines, sliced
1 large ripe mango, peeled and cut into 1-inch chunks
1 cup blueberries
2 cups orange juice
¼ cup amaretto *or* ½ teaspoon almond extract
2 tablespoons sugar
   Fresh mint (optional)

1. Combine peaches, nectarines, mango and blueberries in large bowl.

2. Whisk orange juice, amaretto and sugar in small bowl until sugar is dissolved. Pour over fruit mixture; toss to coat. Marinate 1 hour at room temperature, gently stirring occasionally. Garnish with fresh mint.

Pumpkin Mousse
Makes 6 servings

1 cup milk
1 package (4-serving size) butterscotch instant pudding and pie
   filling mix
1 can (15 ounces) solid-pack pumpkin
¼ teaspoon ground cinnamon
   Pinch ground ginger
   Pinch ground cloves
1 container (8 ounces) whipped topping, divided
2 tablespoons chopped crystallized ginger (optional)

1. Whisk milk and pudding mix in large bowl. Add pumpkin, cinnamon, ground ginger and cloves; whisk until well blended.

2. Reserve ¼ cup whipped topping for garnish. Fold remaining whipped topping into pudding mixture. Refrigerate 1 hour or until set. Top with a dollop of reserved whipped topping and crystallized ginger before serving.

Summertime Fruit Medley

Crunch Peach Cobbler

Makes about 6 servings

⅓ cup plus 1 tablespoon granulated sugar, divided
1 tablespoon cornstarch
1 can (29 ounces) *or* 2 cans (16 ounces each) cling peach slices in
    juice, drained and ¾ cup juice reserved
½ teaspoon vanilla
2 cups all-purpose flour, divided
½ cup packed light brown sugar
⅓ cup old-fashioned or quick oats
¼ cup (½ stick) butter, melted
½ teaspoon ground cinnamon
½ teaspoon salt
½ cup cold shortening
4 to 5 tablespoons cold water
    Whipped cream (optional)

1. Combine ⅓ cup granulated sugar and cornstarch in small saucepan. Slowly stir in reserved ¾ cup peach juice. Cook and stir over low heat until thickened. Stir in vanilla. Set aside.

2. Combine ½ cup flour, brown sugar, oats, butter and cinnamon in small bowl; stir until mixture forms coarse crumbs. Set aside.

3. Preheat oven to 350°F. Combine remaining 1½ cups flour, remaining 1 tablespoon granulated sugar and salt in medium bowl. Cut in shortening with pastry blender or two knives until mixture forms pea-sized pieces. Sprinkle water, 1 tablespoon at a time, over flour mixture. Toss lightly with fork after each addition until mixture holds together. Press together to form ball.

4. Roll dough into 10-inch square, ⅛ inch thick. Fold dough in half, then in half again. Carefully place folded dough in center of 8-inch square baking dish. Unfold and press onto bottom and about 1 inch up sides of dish. Arrange peaches over crust. Pour reserved peach sauce over peaches. Sprinkle with reserved crumb topping.

5. Bake 45 minutes. Serve warm or at room temperature with whipped cream.

Crunch Peach Cobbler

Wacky Watermelon
Makes 12 servings

4 cups diced seedless watermelon
¼ cup strawberry fruit spread
2 cups vanilla frozen yogurt
3 tablespoons mini chocolate chips, divided

1. Place 2 cups watermelon and fruit spread in blender; pulse on low until smooth. Add remaining 2 cups watermelon; pulse again until smooth. Add frozen yogurt, 1 cup at a time, pulsing until smooth after each addition.

2. Pour mixture into 8×4-inch loaf pan; freeze 2 hours or until mixture begins to harden around edge of pan. Stir well until mixture is smooth and slushy. Stir in 2 tablespoons chocolate chips. Smooth top of mixture with back of spoon. Sprinkle evenly with remaining 1 tablespoon chocolate chips. Cover pan with foil; freeze 6 hours or overnight.

3. To serve, place pan in warm water briefly; invert onto cutting board. Let stand 5 minutes on cutting board to soften slightly. Cut loaf into slices. Serve immediately.

4. Wrap any leftover slices individually in plastic wrap. Store in freezer.

Wacky Watermelon

Grilled Pineapple with Ice Cream and Chocolate

Makes 4 servings

2 tablespoons cinnamon-sugar*
¼ teaspoon allspice
8 (¾-inch-thick) slices fresh pineapple
Vanilla ice cream or any flavor
Chocolate, fudge, butterscotch or caramel sauce, heated

*To make cinnamon-sugar, combine 2 tablespoons sugar with 1 teaspoon cinnamon.

1. Combine cinnamon-sugar with allspice. Sprinkle pineapple slices with spice mixture. Grill over medium-low heat 7 minutes or until golden brown, turning once.

2. Top pineapple with ice cream and drizzle with warm chocolate sauce.

S'mores Fondue

Makes 8 to 12 servings

1 pound milk chocolate, chopped
2 jars (7 ounces each) marshmallow creme
⅔ cup half-and-half
2 teaspoons vanilla
4 bananas
1 cup mini marshmallows
24 graham crackers
24 strawberries

SLOW COOKER DIRECTIONS
1. Combine chocolate, marshmallow creme, half-and-half and vanilla in slow cooker. Cover; cook on LOW 1½ to 3 hours, stirring after 1 hour. Sprinkle fondue with mini marshmallows.

2. Peel bananas and cut into ½-inch slices. Serve fondue with banana slices, graham crackers and strawberries.

Grilled Pineapple with Ice Cream and Chocolate

Upside-Down Apple Tart

Makes 6 servings

1 sheet (half of 17-ounce package) frozen puff pastry
1½ tablespoons butter, softened
½ cup packed brown sugar
5 to 6 large apples (about 3½ pounds), peeled, cored and cut into thick wedges

1. Thaw puff pastry according to package directions. Unfold on cutting board and trim into 8-inch circle. Place on baking sheet and refrigerate until needed.

2. Spread butter on sides and bottom of 8-inch cast iron skillet. Spread sugar evenly over bottom. Arrange apple wedges in tight concentric circles in prepared skillet. Wedges should extend over top of skillet by about 1 inch. (They will shrink as they cook.)

3. Cook undisturbed over medium heat 15 minutes or until sugar bubbles up. Preheat oven to 375°F.

4. Place skillet in oven on large sheet of foil to catch drips. Bake 15 to 20 minutes or until apples begin to shrink.

5. Carefully remove skillet from oven and place dough over top, tucking dough around edge of apples. Bake 15 to 20 minutes or until pastry is puffed and browned.

6. Remove skillet to wire rack and cool 15 minutes. Place serving plate over top of skillet. Invert tart onto plate.

Extras: Serve tart with whipped cream or ice cream.

Upside-Down Apple Tart

Fresh Peach Slices

Makes 20 servings

CRUST

4 cups all-purpose flour
2 tablespoons granulated sugar
1 teaspoon salt
1¼ cups (2½ sticks) unsalted butter, thinly sliced
1 to 1⅛ cups cold milk

FILLING

12 cups thinly sliced peaches (about 12 to 16 medium ripe peaches)
1 cup granulated sugar
½ to ⅔ cup all-purpose flour*
¼ cup packed brown sugar
1 tablespoon lemon juice
2 teaspoons ground cinnamon
¼ teaspoon salt
⅛ teaspoon ground allspice
2 tablespoons unsalted butter, thinly sliced

GLAZE

½ cup powdered sugar
1½ to 2 tablespoons milk
¼ teaspoon vanilla

Flour amount will depend on peaches; use more flour for juicy peaches.

1. For crust, combine flour, sugar and salt in large bowl. Cut in butter with pastry blender or two knives until mixture resembles coarse crumbs. Add milk, ¼ cup at a time, stirring dough gently until mixture comes together. Separate one third dough and form into ball; form remaining two thirds dough into another ball. Rest dough 15 minutes. Roll out larger ball on lightly floured surface into 17×14-inch rectangle. Ease dough over rolling pin and transfer into 13×9-inch baking pan, covering bottom and sides. Set aside.

2. Preheat oven to 400°F. For filling, combine peaches, granulated sugar, flour, brown sugar, lemon juice, cinnamon, salt and allspice in large bowl. Spoon fruit evenly into pastry-lined pan; dot with butter.

continued on page 256

Fresh Peach Slice

Fresh Peach Slices, continued

3. Roll out remaining dough to 13×9-inch rectangle. Place over fruit. Pinch edges of bottom crust over top crust, forming a ridge. Seal, cutting off and discarding excess dough. Cut 2 or 3 vents into top crust.

4. Place pan on baking sheet to catch any drips. Bake 1 hour or until crust is golden brown and filling is bubbling. Cool in pan on wire rack 1 hour.

5. For glaze, combine powdered sugar, 1½ tablespoons milk and vanilla in small bowl. Add more milk, if necessary, to reach drizzling consistency. Drizzle glaze over top of dessert; allow to set 30 minutes. Cut into squares.

Chocolate Fruit Tarts
Makes 6 tarts

1 refrigerated pie crust (half of 15-ounce package)
1¼ cups prepared chocolate pudding (about 4 snack-size pudding cups)
Fresh sliced strawberries, raspberries or blackberries

1. Preheat oven to 450°F. Spray back of standard (2½-inch) muffin pan with nonstick cooking spray. Let pie crust stand at room temperature 15 minutes.

2. Unroll crust onto clean work surface; cut out 6 circles with 4-inch round cookie cutter. Place crust circles over backs of alternate muffin cups, pinching crust into 5 or 6 pleats around sides of cups. (Press firmly to hold crust in place.) Prick bottom and sides with fork.

3. Bake about 8 minutes or until golden brown. Carefully remove tart shells from backs of muffin cups; cool completely on wire rack.

4. Fill each tart shell with about 3 tablespoons pudding; arrange fruit on top.

Chocolate Fruit Tarts

Rustic Plum Tart

Makes one 9-inch tart

¼ cup (½ stick) plus 1 tablespoon butter, divided
3 cups plum wedges (about 6 medium, see Tip)
¼ cup granulated sugar
½ cup all-purpose flour
½ cup old-fashioned or quick oats
¼ cup packed brown sugar
1 tablespoon chopped crystallized ginger
½ teaspoon ground cinnamon
¼ teaspoon salt
1 egg
1 teaspoon water
1 refrigerated pie crust (half of 15-ounce package)

1. Preheat oven to 425°F. Line baking sheet with parchment paper.

2. Melt 1 tablespoon butter in large skillet over high heat. Add plums; cook and stir 3 minutes or until plums are softened. Stir in granulated sugar; cook 1 minute or until juices have thickened. Remove from heat; set aside.

3. Combine flour, oats, brown sugar, ginger, cinnamon and salt in medium bowl. Cut in remaining ¼ cup butter with pastry blender or two knives until mixture resembles coarse crumbs.

4. Beat egg and water in small bowl. Unroll pie crust on prepared baking sheet. Brush crust lightly with egg mixture. Sprinkle with ¼ cup oat mixture, leaving 2-inch border around edge of crust. Spoon plums over oat mixture, leaving juices in skillet. Fold crust edge up around plums, overlapping as necessary. Sprinkle with remaining oat mixture. Brush edge of crust with egg mixture.

5. Bake 25 minutes or until golden brown. Cool slightly before serving.

 Tip: For this recipe, use dark reddish-purple plums and cut the fruit into 8 wedges.

Rustic Plum Tart

Vanilla-Strawberry Cupcakes

Makes 28 cupcakes

  2 cups all-purpose flour
  2 teaspoons baking powder
  ¼ teaspoon salt
1¾ cups granulated sugar
  ¾ cup (1½ sticks) butter, softened, divided
  ¾ cup milk
3½ teaspoons vanilla, divided
  3 egg whites
  ½ cup strawberry preserves
  1 package (8 ounces) cream cheese, chilled and cut into cubes
  2 cups powdered sugar
  1 to 1½ cups sliced fresh strawberries

1. Preheat oven to 350°F. Lightly grease 28 standard (2½-inch) muffin cups or line with paper baking cups.

2. Combine flour, baking powder and salt in medium bowl; mix well. Beat granulated sugar and ½ cup butter in large bowl with electric mixer at medium speed 1 minute. Add milk and 1½ teaspoons vanilla; beat at low speed 30 seconds. Gradually beat in flour mixture; beat at medium speed 2 minutes. Add egg whites; beat 1 minute.

3. Spoon batter into prepared muffin cups, filling half full. Drop 1 teaspoon preserves on top of batter in each cup; swirl into batter with toothpick. Bake 20 to 22 minutes or until toothpick inserted into centers comes out clean. Cool cupcakes in pans on wire racks 10 minutes. Remove to racks; cool completely. (At this point, cupcakes may be frozen up to 3 months. Thaw at room temperature before frosting.)

4. Combine cream cheese, ¼ cup butter and 2 teaspoons vanilla in small bowl with electric mixer at medium speed until blended. Add powdered sugar; beat just until incorporated. (Do not overmix or frosting will be too soft to spread.)

5. Frost cupcakes; top with strawberries. Serve immediately or refrigerate up to 8 hours before serving.

Vanilla-Strawberry Cupcakes

Easy Raspberry Ice Cream
Makes 3 servings

1¾ cups frozen unsweetened raspberries
2 to 3 tablespoons powdered sugar
½ cup whipping cream

Place raspberries in food processor. Process 15 seconds or until finely chopped. Add sugar; process until smooth. Add cream; process until well blended. Serve immediately.

Slow Cooker Peach-Oat Crumble
Makes about 8 servings

8 cups frozen sliced peaches, thawed and juice reserved
¾ cup packed brown sugar, divided
1½ tablespoons cornstarch
1 tablespoon lemon juice (optional)
1½ teaspoons vanilla
½ teaspoon almond extract
1 cup quick oats
¼ cup all-purpose flour
¼ cup granulated sugar
1 teaspoon ground cinnamon
¼ teaspoon salt
½ cup (1 stick) cold butter, cut into small pieces

SLOW COOKER DIRECTIONS
1. Lightly coat inside of 4½-quart slow cooker with nonstick cooking spray.

2. Combine peaches with juice, ½ cup brown sugar, cornstarch, lemon juice, if desired, vanilla and almond extract in medium bowl. Toss until peaches are well coated. Transfer to slow cooker.

3. Combine oats, flour, remaining ¼ cup brown sugar, granulated sugar, cinnamon and salt in medium bowl. Cut in butter with pastry blender or two knives until mixture resembles coarse crumbs. Sprinkle over peaches. Cover; cook on HIGH 1½ hours or until bubbly at edge. Remove insert and cool 20 minutes before serving.

Easy Raspberry Ice Cream

Sweet Treats

Pumpkin-Oatmeal Raisin Cookies

Makes 4 dozen cookies

 2 cups all-purpose flour
1⅓ cups quick or old-fashioned oats
 2 teaspoons pumpkin pie spice
 1 teaspoon baking soda
 ½ teaspoon salt
 1 cup (2 sticks) butter or margarine, softened
 1 cup packed brown sugar
 1 cup granulated sugar
 1 cup LIBBY'S® 100% Pure Pumpkin
 1 egg
 1 teaspoon vanilla extract
 ¾ cup chopped walnuts
 ¾ cup raisins

PREHEAT oven to 350°F. Lightly grease baking sheets.

COMBINE flour, oats, pie spice, baking soda and salt in medium bowl. Beat butter, brown sugar and granulated sugar in large mixer bowl until light and fluffy. Add pumpkin, egg and vanilla extract; mix well. Add flour mixture; mix well. Stir in nuts and raisins. Drop by rounded tablespoons onto prepared baking sheets.

BAKE for 14 to 16 minutes or until cookies are lightly browned and set in centers. Cool on baking sheets for 2 minutes; remove to wire racks to cool completely.

Cherry-Filled Hearts

Makes 8 servings

½ package (about 17 ounces) frozen puff pastry sheets (1 sheet),
thawed
1 egg yolk
1 teaspoon water
1 can (21 ounces) cherry pie filling
¼ teaspoon almond extract
2½ cups whipped topping
½ cup hot fudge topping, heated

1. Preheat oven to 400°F.

2. Unfold puff pastry sheet on lightly floured surface. Cut out 8 hearts using 3-inch cookie cutter. Place on ungreased baking sheet.

3. Combine egg yolk and water in small bowl; beat lightly with fork until well blended. Brush evenly onto pastry cutouts, covering completely. Bake 10 to 12 minutes or until golden brown. Remove to wire rack; cool completely.

4. Meanwhile, combine pie filling and extract in medium saucepan. Cook and stir over low heat until heated through. Cool slightly.

5. Carefully split each heart horizontally in half. Place bottom halves of hearts on plates; top evenly with pie filling mixture and whipped topping. Replace top halves of hearts; drizzle with fudge topping.

Cherry-Filled Hearts

Banana Split Ice Cream Sandwiches

Makes 9 servings

1 package (about 16 ounces) refrigerated chocolate chip cookie dough
2 ripe bananas, mashed
½ cup strawberry jam, divided
4 cups strawberry ice cream, softened
Hot fudge topping
Whipped cream
9 maraschino cherries

1. Let dough stand at room temperature about 15 minutes. Preheat oven to 350°F. Lightly grease 13×9-inch baking pan.

2. Beat dough and bananas in large bowl with electric mixer at medium speed until well blended. Spread dough evenly in prepared pan and smooth top. Bake about 22 minutes or until edges are light brown. Cool completely in pan on wire rack.

3. Line 8-inch square baking pan with foil or plastic wrap, allowing 1-inch overhang. Remove cooled cookie from pan; cut in half crosswise. Place 1 cookie half, top side down, in 8-inch pan, trimming edges to fit, if necessary. Spread ¼ cup jam evenly over cookie. Spread ice cream evenly over jam. Spread remaining ¼ cup jam over bottom of remaining cookie half; place jam side down over ice cream. Wrap tightly with foil; freeze at least 2 hours or overnight.

4. Cut into bars and top with hot fudge topping, whipped cream and cherries.

Banana Split Ice Cream Sandwiches

S'mores Bundles
Makes 8 servings

1¼ cups mini marshmallows
1¼ cups semisweet chocolate chips
1¼ cups coarsely crushed graham crackers (5 whole graham crackers)
1 package (about 17 ounces) frozen puff pastry, thawed

1. Preheat oven to 400°F. Combine marshmallows, chocolate chips and graham crackers in medium bowl.

2. Unfold pastry on lightly floured surface. Roll each pastry sheet into 12-inch square; cut into 4 (6-inch) squares. Place scant ½ cup marshmallow mixture in center of each square.

3. Brush edges of pastry squares with water. Bring edges together over filling; twist tightly to seal. Place bundles 2 inches apart on ungreased baking sheets.

4. Bake about 20 minutes or until golden brown. Cool on wire rack 5 minutes; serve warm.

Oat-y Nut Bars
Makes 16 bars

½ cup (1 stick) butter
½ cup honey
¼ cup packed brown sugar
¼ cup corn syrup
2¾ cups quick oats
⅔ cup raisins
½ cup salted peanuts

1. Preheat oven to 300°F. Grease 9-inch square baking pan. Combine butter, honey, brown sugar and corn syrup in medium saucepan over medium heat, stirring until melted. Bring to a boil; boil 8 minutes or until mixture thickens slightly. Stir in oats, raisins and peanuts until well blended. Press evenly into prepared pan.

2. Bake 25 to 30 minutes or until golden brown. Score into 2-inch squares. Cool completely in pan on wire rack. Cut into bars along score lines.

S'mores Bundles

Frosty Chocolate-Cherry Treats

Makes 8 servings

1 package (about 18 ounces) triple chocolate cake mix
1 cup water
1 package (4-serving size) chocolate instant pudding and pie
   filling mix
2 eggs
1 tablespoon instant coffee granules
1 teaspoon vanilla
2 pints cherry chip or chocolate-cherry chip ice cream, softened
5 egg whites
½ cup sugar
¼ teaspoon salt

1. Preheat oven to 350°F. Spray 8 (6-ounce) custard cups with nonstick cooking spray. Place on rimmed baking sheet.

2. Beat cake mix, water, pudding mix, eggs, coffee granules and vanilla in large bowl with electric mixer at low speed 1 minute. Beat at medium speed 2 minutes or until well blended and fluffy (batter will be very thick). Spoon ½ cup batter into each custard cup. Bake 20 to 25 minutes or until toothpick inserted into centers comes out clean. Cool cakes completely; remove from custard cups and return to baking sheet.

3. Place broiler rack 6 inches from heat; preheat broiler. Scoop about ⅓ cup ice cream on top of each cake; place in freezer. Using clean beaters, beat egg whites in medium bowl with electric mixer at high speed 1 to 2 minutes or until foamy. Gradually add sugar and salt; beat about 5 minutes or until stiff peaks form. Spread 1 cup meringue over ice cream scoops to edges of cakes, mounding in centers to create dome shapes.

4. Broil 1 to 2 minutes or until meringue is lightly browned. Serve immediately.

Frosty Chocolate-Cherry Treats

Peanutty Crispy Dessert Cups

Makes 12 servings

⅓ cup creamy peanut butter
2 tablespoons butter
3 cups large marshmallows (5 ounces)
3 cups chocolate-flavored crisp rice cereal
Ice cream or frozen yogurt
Chocolate sauce, colored candies and sprinkles, chopped peanuts,
strawberries and/or maraschino cherries

1. Heat peanut butter and butter in large saucepan over low heat until melted and smooth. Add marshmallows; cook and stir until melted. Remove pan from heat; stir in cereal until well blended and cooled slightly.

2. Scoop mixture evenly into 12 standard (2½-inch) nonstick muffin cups; press into bottoms and up sides of cups.

3. Refrigerate 5 to 10 minutes or until set. Remove cups from pan; fill with ice cream and sprinkle with desired toppings.

Peanutty Crispy Dessert Cups

Zesty Orange Cookie Cups

Makes 4 dozen cookie cups

1 cup (2 sticks) butter, softened
½ cup granulated sugar
2 cups all-purpose flour
2 cups (12-ounce package) NESTLÉ® TOLL HOUSE® Premier White Morsels
2 eggs
1 can (14 ounces) NESTLÉ® CARNATION® Sweetened Condensed Milk
½ to ¾ teaspoon orange extract
1 tablespoon grated orange peel (1 medium orange)

PREHEAT oven to 350°F. Grease 48 mini muffin cups.

BEAT butter and sugar in medium mixer bowl until creamy. Add flour; beat until mixture is evenly moistened, crumbly and can be formed into balls. Shape dough into 1-inch balls. Press each ball onto bottom and up side of prepared muffin cups to form wells. Place *5 morsels* in each cup.

BEAT eggs in medium bowl with wire whisk. Stir in sweetened condensed milk and orange extract. Spoon almost a measuring tablespoon of mixture into each muffin cup, filling about ¾ full.

BAKE for 15 to 17 minutes or until centers are puffed and edges are just beginning to brown. Upon removing from oven, gently run knife around each cup. **While still warm,** top each cup with 8 to 10 morsels (they will soften and retain their shape). Cool completely in pans on wire racks. With tip of knife, remove cookie cups from muffin pans. Top with grated orange peel just before serving. Store in covered container in refrigerator.

Zesty Orange Cookie Cups

Mini S'mores Pies

Makes 6 servings

6 mini graham cracker pie crusts
½ cup semisweet chocolate chips, divided
¾ cup mini marshmallows

1. Preheat oven to 325°F. Place pie crusts on rimmed baking sheet.

2. Divide ¼ cup chocolate chips between pie crusts. Sprinkle marshmallows over chocolate chips. Top with remaining ¼ cup chocolate chips.

3. Bake 3 to 5 minutes or until marshmallows are light golden brown.

Mocha Java Cookies

Makes about 2½ dozen cookies

½ cup granulated sugar
½ cup packed brown sugar
½ cup (1 stick) unsalted butter, softened
1 egg
1½ cups all-purpose flour
2 tablespoons instant espresso powder
1 teaspoon baking soda
½ teaspoon salt
¾ cup semisweet chocolate chips
¾ cup milk chocolate chips
½ cup milk chocolate toffee bits

1. Line cookie sheets with parchment paper.

2. Beat granulated sugar, brown sugar, butter and egg in large bowl with electric mixer at medium speed until blended. Add flour, espresso powder, baking soda and salt; beat just until combined. Stir in chocolate chips and toffee bits (dough will be stiff). Cover and refrigerate dough 1 hour.

3. Preheat oven to 350°F. Shape dough into 2-inch balls. Place on prepared cookie sheets 2 inches apart. Slightly flatten each ball with back of spoon.

4. Bake 7 to 9 minutes or until edges are golden brown. Cool on cookie sheets 5 minutes. Remove to wire racks; cool completely. Store cookies in airtight container.

Mini S'mores Pies

Acknowledgments

The publisher would like to thank the companies listed below for the use of their recipes and photographs in this publication.

The Beef Checkoff

Bob Evans®

Campbell Soup Company

Chef Paul Prudhomme's Magic Seasoning Blends®

Del Monte Foods

Dole Food Company, Inc.

Duncan Hines® and Moist Deluxe® are registered trademarks of Pinnacle Foods Corp.

EAGLE BRAND®

Florida Department of Agriculture and Consumer Services, Bureau of Seafood and Aquaculture

The Hershey Company

Kraft Foods Global, Inc.

Nestlé USA

Ortega®, A Division of B&G Foods, Inc.

Reckitt Benckiser Inc.

Recipes courtesy of the Reynolds Kitchens

Riviana Foods Inc.

Sargento® Foods Inc.

Unilever

Veg•All®

Wisconsin Milk Marketing Board

Index

METRIC CONVERSION CHART

VOLUME MEASUREMENTS (dry)

$^1/_8$ teaspoon = 0.5 mL
$^1/_4$ teaspoon = 1 mL
$^1/_2$ teaspoon = 2 mL
$^3/_4$ teaspoon = 4 mL
1 teaspoon = 5 mL
1 tablespoon = 15 mL
2 tablespoons = 30 mL
$^1/_4$ cup = 60 mL
$^1/_3$ cup = 75 mL
$^1/_2$ cup = 125 mL
$^2/_3$ cup = 150 mL
$^3/_4$ cup = 175 mL
1 cup = 250 mL
2 cups = 1 pint = 500 mL
3 cups = 750 mL
4 cups = 1 quart = 1 L

VOLUME MEASUREMENTS (fluid)

1 fluid ounce (2 tablespoons) = 30 mL
4 fluid ounces ($^1/_2$ cup) = 125 mL
8 fluid ounces (1 cup) = 250 mL
12 fluid ounces (1$^1/_2$ cups) = 375 mL
16 fluid ounces (2 cups) = 500 mL

WEIGHTS (mass)

$^1/_2$ ounce = 15 g
1 ounce = 30 g
3 ounces = 90 g
4 ounces = 120 g
8 ounces = 225 g
10 ounces = 285 g
12 ounces = 360 g
16 ounces = 1 pound = 450 g

DIMENSIONS

$^1/_{16}$ inch = 2 mm
$^1/_8$ inch = 3 mm
$^1/_4$ inch = 6 mm
$^1/_2$ inch = 1.5 cm
$^3/_4$ inch = 2 cm
1 inch = 2.5 cm

OVEN TEMPERATURES

250°F = 120°C
275°F = 140°C
300°F = 150°C
325°F = 160°C
350°F = 180°C
375°F = 190°C
400°F = 200°C
425°F = 220°C
450°F = 230°C

BAKING PAN SIZES

Utensil	Size in Inches/Quarts	Metric Volume	Size in Centimeters
Baking or Cake Pan (square or rectangular)	8×8×2	2 L	20×20×5
	9×9×2	2.5 L	23×23×5
	12×8×2	3 L	30×20×5
	13×9×2	3.5 L	33×23×5
Loaf Pan	8×4×3	1.5 L	20×10×7
	9×5×3	2 L	23×13×7
Round Layer Cake Pan	8×1½	1.2 L	20×4
	9×1½	1.5 L	23×4
Pie Plate	8×1¼	750 mL	20×3
	9×1¼	1 L	23×3
Baking Dish or Casserole	1 quart	1 L	—
	1½ quart	1.5 L	—
	2 quart	2 L	—